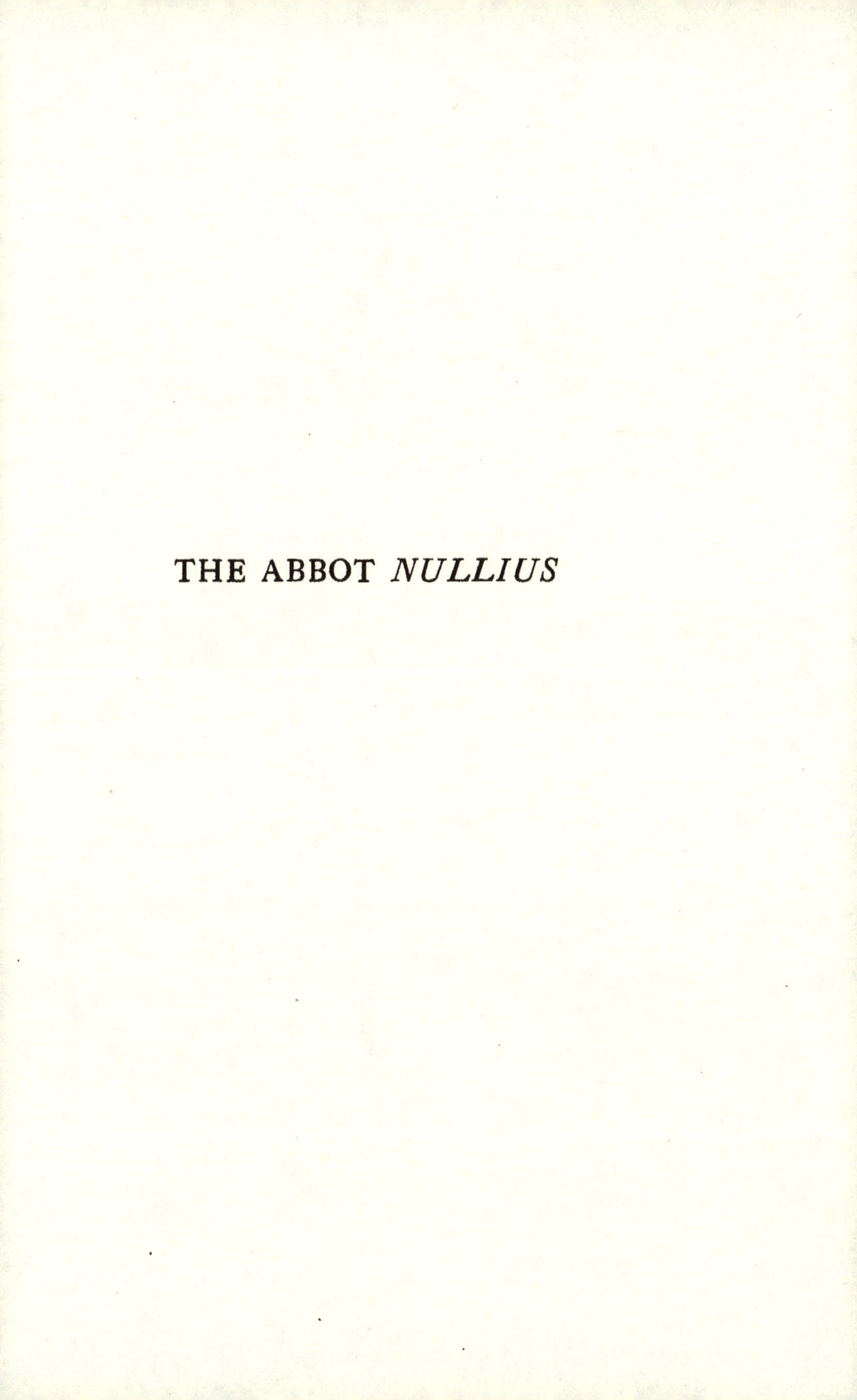

THE ABBOT *NULLIUS*

THE CATHOLIC UNIVERSITY OF AMERICA
CANON LAW STUDIES
No. 173

The Abbot *Nullius*

BY

REV. MATTHEW A. BENKO, O.S.B., J.C.L.
Priest of the Archabbey of St. Vincent, Latrobe, Pa.

A DISSERTATION

Submitted to the Faculty of the School of Canon Law of the Catholic University of America in Partial Fulfillment of the Requirements for the Degree of

DOCTOR OF CANON LAW

THE CATHOLIC UNIVERSITY OF AMERICA PRESS
WASHINGTON, D.C.
1943

NIHIL OBSTAT

Hieronymus D. Hannan, A.M., LL.B., S.T.D., J.C.D.,
Censor Deputatus.

Washingtonii, die 21 maii, 1943.

IMPRIMI POTEST

✠ Alfridus Koch, O.S.B.,
Archiabbas Sancti Vincentii,

Archiabbatia Sancti Vincentii, Latrobe, Pa., die 22 maii, 1943.

IMPRIMATUR

✠ Hugo Carolus Boyle,
Episcopus Pittsburgensis,

Pittsburgi, die 22 maii, 1943.

PRINTED IN THE UNITED STATES OF AMERICA
BY
The Archabbey Press • Latrobe, Pennsylvania

Reverendissimo et Amplissimo Domino,

Archiabbati Alfrido,

Patri benevolo studiorumque fautori

hoc opusculum dicat auctor

TABLE OF CONTENTS

CHAPTER III

CHAPTER IV

CHAPTER V

CHAPTER VI

INTRODUCTION

The Church, ever solicitous about the welfare of her spiritual children, always sees to it that none of her flock are without a shepherd. As the Church expanded and the number of the faithful increased, the bestowal of this care became more difficult. Hence Rome repeatedly entrusted the care of souls to ordinary priests, frequently religious missionaries, who were not consecrated bishops. This usually happened in sparsely settled territories where only missionaries labored among the faithful. In places where the monastic orders were firmly established, the faithful were sometimes placed under the care of the superior of the monastery. Sometimes this was done out of necessity, sometimes it was granted as a privilege. From such instances there arose the institute known today as the abbacy or prelacy *nullius dioecesis*, a territory separate and distinct from any diocese, directly governed by an abbot or prelate *nullius*. In some instances this institute resulted from a further extension of monastic exemption, when the religious superior, besides exemption, acquired certain episcopal privileges.

The legislation concerning the abbacy and prelacy *nullius* was rather vague in pre-Code law. Most of it had to be gleaned from particular papal documents which granted specific privileges. In the Code, however, the legislation was made quite definite, in canons 319 to 327. The meager number of references to the old law under these canons shows that the Code has evolved almost a new legislation in this respect, based largely on a few fundamental papal constitutions, especially those of Pope Benedict XIV (1740–1758).

Canons 319 to 327 will, therefore, constitute the matter for consideration in this dissertation. Though the specific purpose of this work is to consider only the abbot *nullius*, nevertheless quite frequently mention must be made also of the prelate *nullius*. The legislation for both is so closely connected that the Code never mentions the one without the other. Both hold the same ecclesiastical office, and hence every canon that explicitly mentions them uses the phrase *abbas vel praelatus nullius*. Hence, what is said in relation to the one obtains also in relation to the other in all such matters wherein the law is of equal application to both. Whenever the application of the law to them reveals any disparity, then that fact is inherent in the difference that exists between ecclesiastics who belong on the one hand to the religious, and on the other hand to the secular clerical state.

In this dissertation it will always be assumed that the abbot is an acting major superior of an exempt clerical religious order. As a consequence, two compatible exclesiastical officers are vested in the same person. The abbot governs his monastic community as a superior in his own right, and at the same time he rules over a separated territory. Perhaps the most striking fact about such an abbot is that, besides being included under the term *ordinarius* according to canon 198, § 2, he is also included under the term *ordinarius loci* of canon 198, § 1, and under the term *episcopus* according to canon 215, § 2. Hence, besides his duties and privileges as a major religious superior or abbot in his own right, he has also the duties and privileges, to a very appreciable extent, of a bishop. He exercises an ordinary jurisdiction over his monks as his religious subjects, and at the same time exercises a diocesan jurisdiction over them and over all the clergy and laity residing in his separated territory as well.

Another principle must be kept well in mind, and that is the principle of canon 215, § 2. This canon rules that in law the word "diocese" includes also an abbacy or prelacy *nullius*, and the word "bishop" includes also the abbot or prelate *nullius*, unless the nature of the legislation or its context should demand otherwise. Many of the rights and duties of these abbots and prelates are deduced from canons which legislate for the diocesan bishop. These canons need to be explained, then, in conjunction with canon 215, § 2. As a fundamental principle it can be stated that usually the rights, duties, and privileges which the canons grant to a bishop by reason of his office are also applicable to prelates and abbots *nullius*. But the rights, duties, and privileges that accrue to a bishop in view of his episcopal consecration, and not in view of his office as diocesan bishop, are not applicable to such prelates and abbots.

The writer wishes to express his gratitude and deepest appreciation to the Right Reverend Alfred Koch, O.S.B., Archabbot of Saint Vincent Archabbey, Latrobe, Pennsylvania, for the opportunity of advanced study, and to the Faculty of the School of Canon Law of the Catholic University of America for their profitable instruction and generous assistance. The writer also feels greatly indebted to the Rev. Anselm Biggs, O.S.B., of Belmont Abbey *Nullius*, Belmont, North Carolina, for the authentic transcript of the original document of the confirmation of the election of the Most Illustrious and Very Reverend Vincent Taylor, O.S.B., Abbot *Nullius* of the same abbey.

CHAPTER I

THE ABBOT *NULLIUS*

ARTICLE I. TERMINOLOGY

In the old law, and among the authors who wrote before the promulgation of the Code, the subordinate prelate was always considered inferior to the bishop.[1] The Council of Trent also adhered to this principle, and considered an abbot *nullius* as inferior to the bishop.[2] According to these authors a subordinate prelate was a cleric who lacked episcopal consecration, but who exercised a quasi-episcopal jurisdiction over the churches and people subject to him.[3] Their whole approach in the matter was from the viewpoint of the power of orders. Major prelates were those who had received episcopal consecration, while the subordinate prelates lacked this consecration, and hence were looked upon as being inferior to the bishops. Because of this outlook these authors usually treated of subordinate prelates after their treatise on bishops, and immediately before the treatise on pastors.[4] Modern authors, although they generally follow the arrangement of the Code, still frequently refer to subordinate prelates as being inferior to the bishop inasmuch as they lack episcopal consecration.[5]

[1] Bouix, *Tractatus de Episcopo* (Parisiis, 1859), I, 532; Petra, *Commentaria ad Constitutiones Apostolicas* (Venetiis, 1729), ad const. IV Callisti III, sect. 1, n. 2 (V, 50); Reiffenstuel, *Jus Canonicum Universum* (6 vols. in 5, Romae, 1831–1835), Lib. I, tit. XXXI, § 1, n. 15; Schmalzgrueber, *Jus Ecclesiasticum Universum* (12 vols., Romae, 1843–1845), lib. I, pars IV, tit. XXXIII, § 1, n. 1; Tamburini, *De Jure Abatum et Aliorum Praelatorum ... Episcopis Inferiorum* (3 vols., Coloniae Agrippinae, 1691), tom. I, disput. I, quaes. VI, n. 3; Wernz, *Jus Decretalium*, II (Romae, 1899), 1017. Cf. also c. 1, D. XXI; *glossa* in c. 4, *de sententia excommunicationis*, V, 11, in VI°.

[2] Conc. Trident., sess. XXIII, *de ref.*, c. 10; sess. XXIV, *de ref.*, c. 9.

[3] Wernz, *Ius Decretalium*, II, 1018.

[4] E.g., Wernz, *loc. cit.*

[5] Wernz-Vidal, *Ius Canonicum*, II (ed. altera, Romae: apud Aedes Univ. Gregorianae, 1928), 601.

The Code, however, has completely deviated from the old law, and has changed the outlook on subordinate prelates through the adoption of a new meaning for the term *praelatus inferior*. It teaches that two grades of hierarchical jurisdiction originate in Divine Law, the Papacy and the Episcopacy. All other jurisdictions in the Church are of ecclesiastical origin, and merely participate in the powers either of the Papacy or of the Episcopacy.[6] Hence the second book of the Code further corroborates this principle in its rubrics to Titles VII and VIII. The rubric of Title VII reads: *De suprema potestate deque iis qui eiusdem sunt ecclesiastico iure participes.* The rubric of Title VIII is worded: *De potestate episcopali deque iis qui de eadem participant.* The last chapter of Title VII deals with subordinate prelates in general. But all the canons in this chapter (Chapter 10 of Title VII), except the very last one (can. 328), deal with the type of subordinate prelate known as the *abbas vel praelatus nullius.*

As a result of these principles it is to be noticed that the treatise on subordinate prelates is placed before the treatise on bishops. In its very logical descending order the Code places the subordinate prelates into the last group of those who participate in papal jurisdiction. The bishops, on the other hand, in accord with the principle of canon 108, § 3, form a new group which, besides the bishops, includes all those who participate in the episcopal jurisdiction. Nowhere in this second group is mention made of subordinate prelates as being inferior to the bishop. It therefore becomes obvious that the Code's whole approach is from a jurisdictional standpoint,[7] and not from the standpoint of the power of orders, as among the pre-Code authors.

Hence two significations of the term *praelatus inferior* must be mentioned. The first, from the standpoint of orders, where-

[6] Can. 108, § 3.

[7] Toso, *Ad Codicem Iuris Canonici Commentaria Minora* (3 toms. in I; tom. I, Romae, Tiferni Tiberini ex offic. Typogr. Vinciana, 1921; Toms. II–III [pars 1–2], Romae, Ephemeridis *Jus Pontificium* cura et impensis, 1923–1927), II, 5. Henceforth cited as *Commentaria.* Toso is one of the few authors who emphasizes the point of jurisdictional approach.

by a subordinate prelate is one who has not received episcopal consecration. The second, from the standpoint of jurisdiction, whereby a subordinate prelate is one who partakes of the papal jurisdiction. Only this second meaning has been adopted, and it seems coined by the Code.

Consequently, because of the arrangement of the Code[8] the term *praelatus inferior* (subordinate prelate) can have only one meaning. Wherever the term occurs in the Code, it is always used in its strict canonical sense, namely of a prelate partaking of papal jurisdiction. From this point of view, which is the Code's point of view, a subordinate prelate is not necessarily inferior to the bishop.[9] Furthermore, since the Code treats of the abbot and prelate *nullius* only under the heading of subordinate prelates,[10] the terms *praelatus inferior* and *abbas vel praelatus nullius* can readily and for practical purposes be looked upon as synonymous.

Since the Code uniformly speaks of an abbot or prelate *nullius*, these terms must next be defined. In the old law, the word "abbot"[11] implied a dignity and an office with jurisdiction. There existed secular as well as religious abbots, but the term in its earliest use was applied to the religious superior of the Benedictine monks.[12] The Code does not explicitly de-

[8] Can. 108, § 3, together with Titles VII–VIII of Book II.

[9] Wernz-Vidal (*Ius Canonicum,* II, 601) do not seem fully to comprehend the Code's strict meaning of the term *praelatus inferior*. "Appellatio autem inferioris, his Praelatis data, videtur dicere respectum ad Praelatos charactere episcopali insignitos (ideoque maiores) . . .". Chelodi (*Ius de Personis,* ed. altera, Tridenti: Libr. edit. Tridentum, 1927) places his treatise on subordinate prelates after his treatise on bishops, adhering to the arrangement of pre-Code authors.

[10] The last canon of chapter 10 (canon 328) excludes other subordinate prelates from the Code by stating that they are to be governed by special regulations of the papal household.

[11] For an etymology of the word, and a good discussion on the abbatial dignity and office, cf. Tamburini, *De Jure Abbatum,* tom. I, disput. I sqq. Cf. also Molitor, *Religiosi Iuris Capita Selecta* (Ratisbonae: ex typis Friderici Pustet, 1909), p. 396; Schaefer, *De Religiosis* (3. ed., Romae: Typis Polyglottis Vaticanis, 1940), n. 160 sqq.

[12] *Regula Sancti Benedicti,* caput. II.

fine the term, but always uses it in connection with religious.[13] Hence, as already mentioned in the introduction, the word "abbot" as used in this dissertation will always signify a major religious superior in charge of a monastery known as an abbey, which as a general rule is a Benedictine abbey.

The Code, however, does define the term "prelate." According to canon 110 a prelate in the strict sense is a cleric, either religious or secular, who enjoys ordinary jurisdiction which is exercisable in the external forum. In the broader sense a prelate may be any cleric holding merely an honorary title, as for instance a monsignor. The prelate *nullius* therefore will always be a prelate in the strict sense. The two concepts may be combined in a simple ecclesiastic, as in the case where a monsignor is granted the jurisdiction of a prelate *nullius*.

There yet remains for explanation the word "*nullius*." The term will be quite clear if the reader remembers that the word "*dioecesis*" is understood in the phrase. The full phrase should read *abbas vel praelatus nullius dioecesis*. It is not clear when the phrase originated. The expression does not occur in the *Corpus Iuris Canonici*, but appears twice in this technical sense in the decrees of the Council of Trent (1545–1563).[14]

After the Council of Trent authors adopted the phrase, and it came to mean a territory completely segregated from an existing diocese. The word *dioecesis* was frequently dropped, and only the word *nullius* was retained in this technical sense. The Code then adopted the term,[15] and used it in relation to a territory completely independent of and separated from any diocesan territory. When used in this technical sense, the word *nullius* is always italicized in the Code.

[13] Abbas Primas: Cans. 223, 4°; 488, 8°; 501 § 3; 510. Abbas superior congregationis monasticae: Cans. 223, 4°; 286, § 4; 488, 8°; 501, § 3; 510; 516, § 1; 655, § 1; 1579, § 2; 1594, § 4. Abbas monasterii sui iuris: Cans. 488, 8°; 647, § 1; 896. Abbas regiminis: Cans. 358, § 1, 8°; 625; 964, 1°. Abbas localis: Cans. 1579, § 1; 1594, § 4. Abbas benedictus: Can. 811, § 2. Abbas *nullius*: Cans. 319–327, and others.

[14] Cf. note 2.

[15] In canon 319, § 1, the Code uses "... *nullius*, nempe dioecesis, ...". In all other instances the word *nullius* stands unaccompanied with the word *dioecesis*.

The English language has no exact literal equivalent for this expression. The finding of some precise English word that adequately delineates the idea of *nullius* is a matter still highly desired, but as yet unaccomplished. The authors simply speak of an abbot or prelate *nullius*, or refer to them as having quasi-diocesan jurisdiction. For the sake of clarity, this dissertation will adhere to the expression abbot *nullius*.

Article II. Definition and Concept

To understand what is really meant by an abbot or prelate *nullius*, it is not enough to refer to them simply as prelates who have obtained some special rights or privileges from the Holy See. That they have such rights and privileges is certainly true, but the statement applies to all prelates alike. To arrive at a clear and specific concept of the particular character that attaches to prelates and abbots *nullius*, it is necessary to consider briefly the various kinds of exemptions, and then to trace the essential factors and features that characterize these prelates as such in law.

Exemption signifies an immunity from the jurisdiction of a superior to whom one is ordinarily subject according to the norms of law.[16] In regard to religious, exemption signifies a removal from the jurisdiction of the diocesan bishop. By reason of the subject to whom it is granted, exemption is divided into personal, when it is granted directly to the person; local, when it is granted directly to a certain place; mixed, when it is granted to certain persons in a certain place.[17] The local and mixed exemptions, and especially the local exemptions, may again be subdivided into passive, semi-active,[18] and active exemptions. The basis for this subdivision is found in the extent of the exemption, *i.e.*, to what extent it removes a territory

[16] Beste, *Introductio in Codicem* (Collegeville, Minn.: Abbey Press, 1938), p. 417.

[17] Coronata, *Institutiones Iuris Canonici* (5 vols. [Vols. I–II, 2. ed. 1939], Taurini: Marietti, 1933–1939), n. 621; Beste, *loc. cit.*

[18] Beste, *Introductio in Codicem*, p. 418.

from the jurisdiction of the bishop. A passive exemption does not imply the separation of a given territory from a given diocese, whereas an active exemption does.[19] The semi-active exemption, as the word indicates, does not completely separate a given territory from a given diocese, yet it curtails the bishop's jurisdiction in the territory to a greater extent than does passive exemption.

With this subdivision as a basis, authors generally distinguish three types of subordinate prelates.[20] The first type (*species infima*) is represented by those prelates who exercise an ordinary jurisdiction over a certain group of people within the premises of a given place. These prelates enjoy what is known as a passive exemption, *i.e.*, they are removed from the jurisdiction of the bishop, and as a consequence exercise an ordinary jurisdiction over their subjects in a given territory. The bishop's diocesan jurisdiction is curtailed, but only to a certain extent. For in some instances specified by law, the bishop still exercises his jurisdiction over the territory in spite of the passive exemption. The territory itself, however, remains a part of the diocese. An exemple of this type of prelate is the major superior of an exempt clerical religious order.

To the second group (*species media*) belong the prelates who exercise jurisdiction over a determined group of clergy and laity, in given territories, and to the complete exclusion of the local ordinary. These prelates enjoy a semi-active exemption, by which the clergy and laity of certain localities are com-

[19] Coronata, *Institutiones*, n. 621; Molitor, *Religiosi Iuris Capita Selecta*, p. 318; Schaefer, *De Religiosis*, n. 419.

[20] Pre-Code authors: Benedictus XIV, *De Synodo Dioecesana* (2 vols., Parmae, 1764), lib. II, c. XI, n. II, III, IV; Bouix, *De Episcopo*, I, 533–534; De Luca, *Theatrum Veritatis et Iustitiae* (16 vols. in 8, Coloniae Agrippinae, 1706), *De iurisdictione*, disc. I, n. 8; De Prosperis, *De Territorio Separato* (Romae, 1712), quaest. VII, n. 1; Petra, *Commentaria ad Constitutiones Apostolicas*, ad const. IV Callisti III, sect. 1, n. 2 sqq.

Post-Code authors: Baucher, "Abbaye Nullius,"—*Dictionnaire de Droit Canonique* (Paris, 1924 -); Beste, *Introductio in Codicem*, p. 418; Vermeersch-Creusen, *Epitome Iuris Canonici* (I, 6. ed., Romae: H. Dessain, 1937), I, n. 437 (henceforth cited as *Epitome*); Wernz-Vidal, *Ius Canonicum*, II, 600; et alii.

pletely removed from the jurisdiction of the local bishop, but the territory is still a part of the diocese. The difference between the first and second group lies in the curtailment of the bishop's jurisdiction. In the first group the ordinary jurisdiction of the bishop is only partially curtailed, since the law allows him to exercise his jurisdiction in certain instances. In the second group the bishop's jurisdiction is completely curtailed, although the exempt territory is still a part of his diocese. Authors refer to such a territory as being in the diocese, but not pertaining to it.[21] The ordinary of military camps is a prelate of this second type.

The last and highest type of subordinate prelates (*species suprema*) includes those who not only exercise an active jurisdiction over a certain personnel, and to the complete exclusion of the bishop's jurisdiction, but whose territory has been actually separated from an existing diocese in such a way that it is no longer a part of that diocese. Such a territory is referred to as neither being in, nor pertaining to a diocese (*nec in dioecesi, nec de dioecesi*). These prelates enjoy an active exemption, and have a complete episcopal jurisdiction over their independent and separated territory, with the exeption of those powers of orders which come exclusively from episcopal consecration. This third class includes properly the abbot and prelate *nullius*.

From the above, therefore, it is quite evident that the essential factor in constituting an abbacy or prelacy *nullius* is the actual separation of that territory from the diocese of which it formerly formed a part.[22] This principle has been preserved in the Code, as is apparent from canon 319, § 1.

> **"Praelati qui praesunt territorio proprio, separato ab omni dioecesi, cum clero et populo, dicuntur Abbates vel Praelati *nullius*, nempe dioecesis, prout eorum ecclesia dignitate abbatiali vel simpliciter praelatitia gaudet."**

21 "In dioecesi, sed non de dioecesi." Cf. note 20.

22 Bouix, *De Episcopo*, I, 538; De Prosperis, *De Territorio Separato*, quaest. II, n. 18; Fagnanus, *Commentaria in quinque Libros Decretalium* (4 vols., Venetiis, 1697), in c. 19 (*Grave*), X, *de officio iud. ordin.*, I, 31, n. 10; Tamburini, *De Jure Abbatum*, tom. I, disput. XV, quaes. IX, n. 4–6; Petra, *Commentaria*, ad const. IV Callisti III, sect. 1, n. 2.

According to this canon, such subordinate prelates hold ordinary jurisdiction over a territory completely separated from a diocese, and over the people who have a domicile or a quasi-domicile in that territory. The wording of the Code indicates that the essential factor is the separation of the territory, and from this separation flows the ordinary jurisdiction over the clergy and laity living in that territory. Furthermore, the canon simply states "*cum clero et populo.*" This includes every baptized catholic of the Latin rite,[23] whether religious or lay, unless the religious are such as enjoy the exemption of canon 615, or have acquired a special privilege of exemption from the Holy See.

The last part of the first paragraph of canon 319 indicates the difference between an abbot and a prelate when both have quasi-diocesan jurisdiction. An abbot *nullius* is one whose church is endowed with the abbatial dignity. In present times such a church is usually the church of some abbey. But formerly there were churches with the abbatial dignity that did not pertain to an abbey or any other monastery, and their rector was a secular abbot. Such churches generally were at least at one time monastic churches or the churches of canons regular. During turbulent times, in view of the dearth of religious or of canons regular, or even as a result of papal intervention, the secular clergy were substituted, and their superior retained the dignity and office of abbot, and the church itself remained an abbatial church.[24] Today, however, an abbot usually also is a major religious superior, though this status is not absolutely necessary for the appointment of an abbot *nullius.*[25]

[23] The Orientals usually have their own bishops, but when they lack their own bishops they are subject to the Latin ordinary. Under like circumstances they also fall under the jurisdiction of the abbot *nullius*.

[24] Tamburini, *De Jure Abbatum,* tom. I, disp. II, quaes. 6, n. 1; Wernz-Vidal, *Ius Canonicum,* II, 601, nota 25.

[25] "Absolute loquendo, necessarium non videtur abbatem nullius religiosum simul esse debere superiorem religiosum et superiorem religiosum majorem. Utrumque tamen accidit generatim, praecipue in Congregationibus Benedictinorum nigrorum."—Larraona, "Commentarium Codicis,"—*Commentarium pro Religiosis,* IV (1923), 111, note (353), (henceforth abbreviated as *CpR.*).

On the other hand, a prelate with a separated territory is one whose church has some prelatical dignity, as for instance that of a minor basilica. Should the rector of such a church jurisdictionally acquire a separated territory, he would become a prelate with quasi-diocesan jurisdiction. At the present time all the abbots and prelates *nullius* are either abbots or monsignors.[26] The churches which serve these prelates as cathedral churches are usually called quasi-cathedral, or quasi-episcopal churches.[27]

Article III. An Historical Synopsis

A. From the Beginning to the Council of Trent

The history of the abbacies and prelacies in a separated territory quite naturally finds its beginnings in the monastic exemptions. With the numerical increase in exemptions, there came a spontaneous increase in the quality of these privileges. Many privileges granted by the Holy See were interpreted to imply the grant of greater powers than they actually did.[28]

The ninth and tenth centuries are usually the ones indicated by authors as the time when the institute of such abbots and prelates originated. The basis for this belief is found in the writings of Benedict XIV whom most of the authors follow.[29] There is an opinion that Monte Cassino had always been an abbey whose abbot exercised quasi-diocesan jurisdiction. Tamburini and De Prosperis are the foremost defenders of this

[26] *Annuario Pontificio*, pro anno 1940.

[27] Coronata, *Institutiones*, n. 730; Vermeersch-Creusen, *Epitome*, II, n. 476; Beste, *Introductio in Codicem*, p. 556.

[28] C. 18, X, *de privilegiis*, V, 33.

[29] Benedictus XIV, *De Synodo Dioecesana*, lib. XIII, c. IX, n. 2; Benedictus XIV, const. "*Inter multa*," 4 apr. 1747 — *Codicis Juris Canonici Fontes cura Em^{i}. Petri Card. Gasparri editi* (Romae, postea Civitate Vaticana: Typis Polyglottis Vaticanis, 1923–1938), n. 379 (henceforth cited as *Fontes*); *Bullarium Benedicti XIV* (Prati, 1845–1847), II, 213 (henceforth cited as *Bull. Ben. XIV*); Wernz-Vidal, *Ius Canonicum*, II, 598.

Cassinese privilege.[30] Their whole argumentation is based on a Rota decision of 1627.[31] According to this decision, Monte Cassino was at first a bishopric.[32] In 529 Saint Benedict came to Monte Cassino, and from that time on, no bishop had been assigned to the place. Wherefore the abbots of that monastery exercised quasi-diocesan jurisdiction even though they were not consecrated bishops. But the Rota decision narrating these facts seems to be based on a spurious document, at least in part. Tamburini completely cites a document of Pope Zachary (741–752), dated February 18, 748, containing the privileges granted to Monte Cassino,[33] and the Rota narrates some of the privileges granted in this document. However, there is no doubt about the falsification of this document. Kehr reports that the document was composed by Peter the Deacon, whom the Rota calls an archivist of merit,[34] along the lines of a genuine document of Pope Zachary, and from a document of Pope Callistus II (1119–1124), of the year 1122.[35]

30 Tamburini, *De Jure Abbatum,* tom. I, disput. III, quaes. IV, n. 1; De Prosperis, *De Territorio Separato,* quaest. XXIX, n. 10.

31 S.R.R. *Sorana Beneficii,* 8 mart. 1627, *coram R. P. D. Merlino—S.R. Rotae Decisionum Recentiorum Partes Variae* (Romae, 1645–1703), pars V, tom. I, dec. XLV.

32 This fact can actually be substantiated from the presence of Bishop Severus of Monte Cassino at a Council held in Rome in the year 487, at which he was one of the thirty-eight bishops present. Conc. Romanum III (487) — Mansi, VII, 1171.

33 Tamburini, *De Jure Abbatum,* tom. I, disput. III, quaes. IV, n. 5.

34 Cf. note 31.

35 Kehr, Paulus, *Italia Pontificia,* VIII (Regnum Normannorum — Campania [Regesta Romanorum Pontificum], Berolini: apud Weidmannos, 1935), p. 121, n. 22. The authentic document of Callistus II is dated Sept. 16, 1122. Hence Peter the Deacon must have composed this spurious document some time after 1122. A genuine document of Pope Zachary is referred to by the writer Leo (*Auctor Leo*) in the Cassinese Chronicle — *MGH, Scriptores,* tom. VII (folio) (ed. Georgius Heinricus Pertz, Hannoverae, 1846; Únveränderter Neudruck, 1925), 582. In 1225 this document was transcribed by Pope Honorius III (1216–1227) in his grant of privileges to the monastery of Saint Martin in Pannonia. Cf. Kehr, *loc. cit.*; Potthast, *Regesta Pontificum Romanorum* (Berolini, 1874–1875), n. 7405. Pope Gregory IX (1227–1241) later confirmed this document. Gregorius IX, epist. "*Abbati et Conventui Monasterii Casinensis,*" 10 apr. 1231 — Kehr, *loc. cit.*; Potthast, n. 8706;

The privilege of exercising quasi-diocesan jurisdiction was authentically granted to Monte Cassino only in 1122, when Pope Callistus II confirmed the abbey's possessions, and placed the Cassinese territory (*locum ipsum*) with all the appurtenances under the direct control of the Holy See.[36] In 1322 the monastery was raised to the status of a real bishopric, and in 1367 it was again reduced to the state in which it existed before the privilege of 1322, *i.e.* to the status of an abbacy with quasi-diocesan jurisdiction.[37]

Consequently there is no strong, and much less verified basis for asserting that Monte Cassino has always been an abbacy *nullius*. Such a view is obviously weakened by the false document of Peter the Deacon.

The first trace of a territory completely segregated from a diocese is that of the Abbey of Einsiedeln. This Abbey was founded about the year 934.[38] At the end of the same century the Abbey of Martinsberg (Pannonia) became an abbey *nullius*. King Saint Stephen of Hungary founded this abbey and endowed it with many privileges. He claimed that in this territory there never had existed a diocese or an abbey. Consequently he maintained that as founder of this episcopacy and

Auvray, *Les Registres de Grégoire IX* (Paris, 1896), I, p. 394, n. 615. Cf. also Hostiensis, *Commentaria in Decretalium Libros* (Venetiis, 1581) in v. *non valent*, c. 13 (*Cum contingat*), X, *de foro competenti*, II, 2.

[36] Callistus II, const. "*Omnipotenti Deo*," 16 sept. 1122 — *Bullarium Romanum* (ed. Taurinensis, 1857–1872), II, 340 (hereafter cited as *Bull. Rom. Taur.*). The *Bullarium* gives the date of this constitution as 16 Sept. 1123. Cf. Kehr, *Regesta Pontificum Romanorum, Italia Pontificia*, VIII, p. 168, n. 201; Jaffé, *Regesta Pontificum Romanorum* (2. ed. curaverunt Loewenfeld, Kaltenbrunner, Ewald, Lipsiae, 1885–1888), n. 6984 (henceforth referred to as JL, JK, JE). This is the document from which Peter the Deacon composed the false one.

[37] Ioannes XXII, const. "*Supernus Opifex*," 2 maii 1322 — *Bull. Rom. Taur.*, IV, 300; Urbanus V, bulla "*Romanus Pontifex*," 31 mart. 1367 — *Bull. Rom. Taur.*, IV, 524.

[38] *Annuario Pontificio*, pro anno 1940. The date for the founding of Einsiedeln is also given as 937. Cf. Segmuller, "*Einsiedeln*,"—*Lexikon für Theologie und Kirche* (Herder: Freiburg im B., 1930–1938), III, 603 (henceforth abbreviated as *LThK*.).

abbey, he had the right to grant whatever privileges he desired.[39] In 1232 Pope Gregory IX confirmed the privileges granted to this abbey by Saint Stephen.[40]

In the eleventh century the Abbey of Cluny became an abbacy *nullius*. Thomassinus reports that the abbey had been founded in a place that was subject to no one, neither to the emperor nor to a bishop. Consequently he does not hesitate to call it truly an abbacy *nullius*.[41] In 1012 Pope Benedict VIII (1012–1024) declared an excommunication against anyone who trespassed on the liberties of this abbey. The noteworthy point about this letter is that it expressly mentioned the territory.[42] It is to be remembered, however, that when these documents speak of the *locus* of a monastery they not only mean the exact plot of ground on which the abbey stands, but all the land that the monastery actually owned.[43] During these times, the monasteries had extremely large territorial possessions as can be seen from the lengthy enumerations of property as contained in some of the papal documents. Lay people in large

[39] Baronius, *Annales Ecclesiastici* (denuo excusi ... ab A. Theiner, 37 vols., vols. I–XXVIII, Barri-Ducis, 1864–1875; vols. XXIX–XXXVII, Parisiis, 1876–1883), anno 1232, n. 23–24 (henceforth cited as *Annales*); Schermann, "*Martinsberg,*" — *LThK*, VI, 994; Thomassinus, *Vetus et Nova Ecclesiae Disciplina* (Magontiaci, 1787), pars I, lib. III, c. XXVI, n. 7.

[40] Gregorius IX, epist. "*Cum in nostra,*" 6 febr. 1232 — Auvray, *Les Registres de Grégoire IX*, I, 486.

[41] Thomassinus, *Vetus et Nova Ecclesiae Disciplina*, pars 1, lib. III, c. XXXVI, n. 2 sqq.

[42] "Quae libertas a cunctis antecessoribus nostris, qui a conditione ipsius loci in hac Sancta Romana ecclesia fuerunt usque ad nos, scriptis privilegiis, et a praelibatis principibus, datis praeceptis; tam de *ipso loco*, quam de omnibus ad se pertinentibus ... videlicet, monasteriis, cellis, terris cultis et incultis, corroborata et confirmata est ..." — Benedictus VIII, epist. "*Liquidum est,*" 15 sept. 1012 — Mansi, XIX, 325; JL, n. 4007. This privilege was again confirmed in the Synod of Rome of 1015—Mansi, XXIX, 361. Pope St. Leo IX (1049–1054) also confirmed this privilege—Leo IX, epist. "*Convenit apostolico,*" 10 iun. 1049 — *Bull. Rom. Taur.*, I, 583; JL, n. 4317.

[43] S.R.R. *Marsicen. seu Nullius iurisdictionis*, 7 iun. 1700, *coram R.P. D. Muto* — *S.R.R. Decisiones Nuperrimae* (9 vols. in 10, Vol. 10 appendix, Romae, 1751–1763), tom. VI, dec. CCXL, n. 29, 30; This decision is also reported in De Prosperis, *De Territorio Separato*, p. 210, ff.

numbers lived on these monastic possessions in the capacity of serfs with the abbot as their temporal ruler. Consequently when Rome declared such a monastery with all its possessions as exempt, the abbot became also the spiritual head of all in his territory. Just what jurisdictional rights such an abbot could exercise depended largely on his privileges, and the papal documents of exemption. Quite frequently he could even convoke synods, which made him truly an abbot *nullius*.

A letter of Pope Callistus II, who again confirmed the privileges of Cluny, exemplifies this situation. The document not only referred to the place exempted, but very definitely determined and specified the territory within which all the churches, cemeteries, monks and all the laity were directly placed under the jurisdiction of the Holy See. Furthermore, no priest or layman within that territory had to attend any synod except that which was convoked by the Roman Pontiff or by the abbot of Cluny.[44]

During the time of Alexander III (1159–1181) no active exemptions were granted whereby the privileged could exercise jurisdiction. Benedict XIV (1740–1758) declared that all the privileges granted during the reign of Alexander III were only passive exemptions.[45]

Thus the eleventh and twelfth century documents show that the emphasis was laid on territorial exemptions. The grants of exemption which restricted episcopal jurisdiction in earlier centuries had been of a personal character, granting merely passive exemptions. But the later grants of exemptions paid more attention to the territory subject to the monastery, and the people in such a territory became exempt by reason of the exempt territory. The abbots of such territories in some instances even had the right to convoke synods, as was shown in the case of Cluny. If the rights of such abbots were to be subjected to a

[44] Callistus II, bulla "*Religionis monasticae*," 22 febr. 1120—*Bull. Rom. Taur.*, II, 303; JL, n. 6821. This document also contains the names of the popes who had on previous occasions granted privileges to Cluny.

[45] Benedictus XIV, const. "*Apostolicae servitutis*," 14 mart. 1743, nn.12–13 — *Bull. Ben. XIV*, I, 276; *Fontes*, n. 334.

scrutiny in the light of the eighteenth century doctrine, the status of these abbots would be found to fulfill the essential characteristics of abbots *nullius,* inasmuch as they had full jurisdiction over a territory actually separated from an existing diocese.

During the twelfth century friction arose between such abbots and the bishops. At the Council of Rome in 1122, the bishops complained they were almost in complete subjection to the monks.[46] This situation required adjustment. So the law on the one hand prescribed that the privileges and rights of the religious should be observed by the bishops, and on the other hand that exempt religious should desist from certain acts which could be performed only by those who had episcopal consecration.[47]

The great Mendicant Orders, instituted during the thirteenth century, likewise acquired many privileges. These were usually communicated to all the houses and members of a religious group even though originally they had been granted to only one monastery. The result was that nearly every monk or religious was to some extent independent of the local ordinary. New struggles arose between the religious and bishops, and the history of religious in these centuries shows much bitter strife. As a result the popes frequently had to settle disputes between the two factions, so that the period immediately preceding the Council of Trent was characterized by many suppressions of privileges.

During the Great Western Schism (1378–1417) there was inaugurated a period of increasing exemptions. The various pontiffs were perhaps trying to win the religious and collegiate chapters to their cause. This resulted in wholesale revocations

[46] "In hoc synodo episcopi adversus monachos invidia inflammati, coeperunt dicere, nil superesse aliud, nisi ut sublatis virgis et annulis, monachis deservirent . . ." — Mansi, XXI, 271. Substantially the same complaint was raised at the I Lateran Council — Mansi, XXI, 299. Cf. also c. unic., *de excessibus praelatorum,* V, 6, in Clem.

[47] C. 15, X, *de praescriptione,* II, 26; c. 12, X, *de excessibus praelatorum,* V, 31; c. 18, X, *de privilegiis,* V, 33; c. 7, *de privilegiis,* V, 7, in VI°; c. unic., *de excessibus praelatorum,* V, 6, in Clem.

of privileges later on. Pope Boniface IX (1389–1402) revoked all the exemptions he had granted during his pontificate, and declared all the letters granting them as being of absolutely no value.[48] On the grounds of this constitution the collegiate church of Saint Peter near Prague, which Boniface IX had exempted from the jurisdiction of the bishop in 1397, was declared as not possessing this privilege.[49] The most sweeping revocation of exemptions was made during the reign of Pope Martin V (1417–1431) at the Council of Constance at which the Great Western Schism was finally healed. In a bull which the Council approved, the pope revoked all the exemptions granted after the death of Pope Gregory XI, who died in 1378.[50] The few exceptions concerned mostly those exemptions which had been granted before the death of Pope Gregory XI. There had been some doubt as to whether this revocation affected all the exemptions granted during the specified time, or only those granted by the anti-popes. The Rota decided that it affected all the exemptions, whether they had been obtained from the true popes or anti-popes, as long as they were granted after the death of Pope Gregory XI.[51]

[48] Bonifatius IX, const. "*Intenta salutis operibus,*" 22 dec. 1402—partly quoted in S.C.C., *in Pragen.*, 20 nov. 1762—*Thesaurus Resolutionum S.C.C.* (Romae, 1718–1908), XXXI, 232. This response also attests to the authenticity of the papal document.

[49] S.C.C., *in Pragen.*, 20 nov. 1762 — *Thesaurus Resolutionem S.C.C.*, XXXI, 231; Pallottini, *Collectio omnium conclusionum et resolutionum quae in causis propositis apud Sacram Congregationem Cardinalium S. Concilii Tridentini interpretum prodierunt ab ejus institutione anno MDLXIV ad annum MDCCCLX* (Romae, 1868-1893), "Exemptio in genere," n. 5 (Henceforth cited as Pallottini).

[50] Martinus V, bulla "*Attendentes,*" 21 mart. 1418—Mansi, XXVII, 1174; Conc. Constantiense (1418), sess. XLIII, *de exemptionibus,*—Mansi, *loc. cit.*

[51] S.R.R. *Ianuam. Iurisdictionis*, 20 iun. 1611, *coram Illustr. et R.P.D. Bononien*—S.R.R. *Decisionum Recentiorum Partes Variae*, pars II, dec. CCCLV; Petra, *Commentaria ad Constitutiones Apostolicas*, ad const. I Paschalis II, sect. I, n. 23. In 1515 Leo X (1513–1521) condemned some unreasonable exemptions, as he called them. Leo X, const. "*Regimini,*" 4 maii 1515—*Bull. Rom. Taur.*, V, 617; V Conc. Lateranense, sess. X—Mansi, XXXII, 907. Cf. also Bonifatius VIII, bulla "*Super cathedram praeeminentiae,*" 18 febr. 1300—Potthast, *Regesta Pontificum Romanorum*, n. 24913; c. 2, *de sepulturis*, III, 7, in Clem; c. 1, *de sepulturis*, III, 7, in Extravag. com.

With such revocations the Church restricted the exemptions, among which were many territorial privileges of jurisdiction. Most of the exemptions which were restricted were those which had been granted so liberally during the schism. With Pope Martin V the situation was again stabilized.

B. FROM THE COUNCIL OF TRENT TO THE CODE

The Council of Trent (1545–1563) enacted very little explicit legislation regarding the abbots and prelates *nullius.* Its main concern seemed to center about the privilege of passive exemption. Such exemptions were not outlawed by the Council, but certain restrictions were placed on them, as for instance by the subjection of monasteries which had the care of souls to episcopal visitation.[52]

In only two instances was the abbot *nullius* explicitly mentioned. The Council ruled that the churches of such abbots were to be visited by that bishop whose cathedral was nearest these churches.[53] Secondly, the Council forbade prelates to confer tonsure and minor orders on anyone who was not directly subject to them. It further forbade these prelates to grant dimissorial letters, and threatened to punish anyone who transgressed this decree.[54]

Because of the Council of Trent's small amount of legislation in this matter, and because of the revocations of many privileges of exemption before the Council, the question of the exempt territory was again bound to come to the fore during the following centuries. The Council had accepted the institute, and the problem of accurately defining the doctrine on such exemptions was left to the numerous decisions of the Rota and of the Sacred Congregation of the Council. Questions of the rights and duties of abbots *nullius*, and of the proof of special grants or of rights acquired by legal prescription constitute the bulk of the jurisprudential consideration regarding this

[52] Conc. Trident., sess. XXV, *de regularibus*, c. 11.

[53] Conc. Trident., sess. XXIV, *de ref.*, c. 9.

[54] Conc. Trident., sess. XXIII, *de ref.*, c. 10.

matter during subsequent centuries. By far the most prominent problem was the proof of the manner of acquisition of such quasi-diocesan jurisdiction. Especially is the eighteenth century rich in its declarations and decisions regarding prelates and abbots *nullius*.

In the early part of the eighteenth century the Rota was engaged in settling what was perhaps the greatest controversy over an abbacy *nullius*. A dispute arose between the Abbot of Fulda and the Bishop of Würzburg.[55] The decision given on June 28, 1700, favored the abbot. It was conceded that he had quasi-diocesan jurisdiction, and for three reasons:

1) The abbey held an original exemption, equivalent to an original jurisdiction, for it was founded before the episcopal see of Würzburg.
2) The abbey further claimed to enjoy special privileges from the Roman Pontiffs granting the abbot a quasi-diocesan jurisdiction.[56]
3) It further claimed a forty year's prescription *cum titulo colorato*.

In the appeal of 1703 this decision was confirmed, but only in relation to the legal factor of prescription. The factors touching the question of original jurisdiction and papal privilege were excluded. In 1705 the decision was again confirmed, this time on the basis of a papal privilege and prescription, but not on the basis of original jurisdiction. A few months later in the same year a decision favoring the abbey was rendered solely on the basis of legal prescription *cum titulo colorato*. In

[55] For a summary of the various decisions regarding this case, and for references to the Rota decisions, cf. Petra, *Commentaria*, in const. IV Callisti III, sect. III. A report on one decision is found also in De Prosperis, *De Territorio Separato*, p. 303.

[56] Fulda based its claims regarding the possession of an exempt territory especially on the following documents. Zacharias, const. "*Quoniam semper*," (day not given) 751—*Bull. Rom. Taur.*, I, 238; JE, n. 2293; Gregorius IV, const. "*Pontificii nostri*," 15 maii 828 (spurious) — JE, n.† 2569; Sylvester II, const. "*Pontificii nostri*," 31 dec. 999—*Bull. Rom. Taur.*, I, 476; JL, n. 3907; Clemens II, const. "*Cura nos urget*," 31 dec. 1046—*Bull. Rom. Taur.*, I, 373; JL, n. 4134.

the appeal of 1710, almost all the judges agreed in excluding the original jurisdiction. The majority also agreed that the papal privileges contained insufficient evidence for the granting of a quasi-diocesan jurisdiction. All except one of the judges agreed that a prescription *cum titulo colorato* was still a basis upon which the monastery could establish its claim of quasi-diocesan jurisdiction. The bishop however contended that such a prescription did not suffice. He petitioned Pope Clement XI (1700–1721) to appoint a special congregation to settle this point. This he did on August 3, 1718. In 1721 this special congregation declared that such a legal prescription did not suffice to establish proof for the existence of an abbacy *nullius*. It decided that the acquisition of such an abbacy or prelacy required either a special and very definite privilege from the Holy See, or a custom existing from time immemorial, rightly proved, so as to warrant a presumption that at one time a privilege had been granted.[57]

In 1743 Pope Benedict XIV settled a controversy between the bishop of the Diocese of Conversano and the Military Order of Hospitallers of Saint John of Jerusalem concerning the exercise of jurisdiction over the town of Putignano.[58] Pope Benedict XIV adjudicated the disputed territory to the bishop, ruling that the Hospitallers had only a passive exemption. In the constitution

[57] "In Congregatione particulari a SS. Domino Nostro [Clemente XI°] die 3 augusti 1718 specialiter deputata EE. DD. Iudice, Vallemani, ... Ansidei Assessoris Sanctissimae Inquisitionis, et mei infrascripti Secretarii memoratae Cong. Concilii Tridentini Interpretis, et huius quoque Particularis Cong. Secretarii, ut in ea videlicet examinaretur, an ad tramites Sacrorum Canonum, Sacrique praesertim Concilii Tridentini, possit inferior Praelatus territorium separatum et iurisdictionem Ordinariam quasi episcopalem in Clerum et populum cum ipsius Episcopi exclusione in aliquo speciali loco acquirere per quadragenariam praescriptionem una cum titulo colorato: praedicti Eminentissimi Domini et RR. PP. particularem Cong. constituentes ... post maturum et diligentissimum materiae examen unanimiter responderunt, non posse, sed pro acquisitione territorii separati praedictaeque iurisdictionis omnino requiri, aut clarum et undequaque subsistens Apostolicum privilegium, aut consuetudinem immemorabilem cum suis omnibus requisitis rite probatam, per quam Apostolicum privilegium de iure praesumi valeat."—S.C.C., 14 ian. 1721—*Fontes*, n. 3219.

[58] Benedictus XIV, const. "*Apostolicae servitutis*," 14 mart. 1743—*Bull. Ben. XIV*, I, 276; *Fontes*, n. 334.

deciding the matter, it was explained that an exempt territory is acquired either by a special privilege or by immemorial prescription. A *titulus coloratus* together with forty years of peaceful possession did not suffice. It was further emphasized that the wording of the papal decree granting the privilege had to be clear and precise, and not general or in any way ambiguous. This decision corresponded to the ultimate decision in the case of Fulda.

Four years later the same pope settled another controversy, namely, one between the Bishop of Frascati and the Abbot of Saint Mary of Grottaferrata of the Order of Saint Basil.[59] In this case it was decided that the monastery enjoyed only a passive exemption, and hence was declared to exist in the Diocese of Frascati. The ordinary jurisdiction was given to the bishop of that diocese. However, new privileges were granted to the abbot, such as the right to administer confirmation, and also the right to approve confessors for the hearing of seculars' confession.[60]

In the nineteenth century controversies between bishops and prelates *nullius* continued. The Holy See had become loath to grant such privileges, and was trying to keep peace by either restricting or completely abolishing the canonical recognition of such prelates. In France, for instance, all exempt territories were suppressed and a redistribution was made to comprise these territories within dioceses.[61]

In Spain, Pope Pius IX (1846–1878) suppressed all the privileged ecclesiastical jurisdictions. This he did by means of two documents issued on the same day, July 12, 1873. In the first

[59] Benedictus XIV, const. "*Inter multa,*" 4 apr. 1747—*Bull. Ben. XIV*, II, 213; *Fontes*, n. 379.

[60] In 1937 Pope Pius XI (1922–1939) elevated the status of this same monastery to that of an abbacy *nullius*. Pius XI, const. "*Pervetustum Cryptaeferratae Coenobium,*" 26 sept. 1937—*Acta Apostolicae Sedis* (Romae, 1909–), XXX (1938), 183 (hereafter abbreviated as *AAS*). Cf. also *Periodica de re canonica et morali utili praesertim religiosis et missionariis* (Bruges, 1905–), XXVII (1938), 223 (hereafter cited as *Periodica*).

[61] Pius VII, const. "*Qui Christi Domini,*" 29 nov. 1801—*Bullarii Romani Continuatio* (Romae, 1835–1857), XI, 245 (hereafter cited as *Bull. Rom. Cont.*).

document[62] he suppressed the jurisdiction of the four Military Orders of Santiago, Alcantara, Calatrava, and Montesa. These Military Orders had in the course of time acquired many privileges in Spain, both from the kings, and from the Holy See at the request of the kings.[63] The document of Pius IX made reference to the concordat of Sept. 5, 1851, between the Spanish government and the Church. According to this pact, there was to be a redistribution of territory, and all bishoprics and exempt territories were to have new limits. But as the document of Pius IX pointed out, before the Church could comply with this agreement, the Spanish government suppressed the four Military Orders mentioned above. Consequently the pope joined their territory to the adjoining dioceses according to the stipulations of the concordat,[64] but expressly specified that this joining of territory would in no way interfere with any future territorial distribution, should this take place in accord with the aforementioned concordat.

The second document of Pius IX[65] mentioned strives between the episcopal ordinaries and the prelates *nullius*. It referred to the previous document, and stated that since the territory of the Military Orders had been joined to the neighboring dioceses, it seemed unfair to favor in one place what had been suppressed in another. Consequently the pope abolished the privileged ecclesiastical jurisdictions in Spain, and joined all their exempt territories to those of the nearest dioceses. How-

[62] Pius IX, litt. ap. *"Quo gravius,"* 12 iul. 1873—*Acta Sanctae Sedis* (Romae, 1865–1908), VII, 480 (hereafter referred to with the abbreviation *ASS*).

[63] For instance, in 1523 Pope Hadrian VI (1522–1523) allowed the kings of Spain to exercise ecclesiastical administration over some territories through a special tribunal composed of members of the Military Orders. Hadrianus VI, bulla *"Dum intra,"* 4 maii 1523—*Bull. Rom. Taur.*, VI, 13. The document of Pius IX cited above refers to this bull of Hadrian VI, but gives the date as 1521.

[64] "Eadem vero Apostolica auctoritate omnia et singula praedictorum Militarium Ordinum territoria et loca ad eadem quoque modo spectantia iuxta articulum 9 commemoratae Conventionis proximis diocesibus iungimus, aggregamus et incorporamus . . ."—Pius IX, litt. ap. *"Quo gravius,"* 12 iul. 1873—*ASS*, VII, (1872–1873), 482.

[65] Pius IX, litt. ap. *"Quae diversa,"* 12 iul. 1873—*ASS*, VII (1872–1873), 485.

ever, he made five exceptions, in accord with article eleven of the concordat.[66] Besides, the same stipulation was made as in the previous document, namely, that this suppression would in no way interfere with the redistribution of the territory that might take place in the future.

The Vatican Council (1869–1870) had to deal with the vexing problem of exempt territories. Many of the bishops at the Council advocated a complete abrogation of this institute, but this view was not accepted favorably by all.[67] Complaints were raised by those present at the Council. For instance Julius, Archbishop of Lucca, complained about exempt prelates who had some jurisdiction over certain congregations. The Archbishop claimed that these prelates were quite a menace to the episcopal jurisdiction, flaunting their privileges, living pretty much as they pleased, and refusing the corrections of the bishops.[68] The Archbishop of Messina complained about a new limitation of dioceses, which are contained within the confines of others. He was referring to the monastery of Saint Salvator of the Order of Saint Basil, at Messina, where no abbot had been elected for fifty years. The monks were exercising the abbot's jurisdictional rights through an administrator.[69]

Under such conditions it was not to be expected that many abbacies or prelacies *nullius* would be established during the nineteenth century. But in very modern times there has been a great increase in the granting of such territories, especially since the promulgation of the Code. In the *Annuario Pontificio* of 1940, 51 such abbacies and prelacies are listed. Of these, 17 had been established between 1920 and 1930. Twelve were erected between 1930 and 1940.[70]

66 "... excepta et in suo robore manente dumtaxat privilegiata eorum iurisdictione, qui nominatim designati fuerunt in 11° Conventionis articulo mox relato."—Pius IX, "*Quae diversa*," 12 iul. 1873—*ASS*, VII (1872–1873), 488. The document then quotes article eleven of the concordat.

67 Wernz-Vidal, *Jus Canonicum*, II, 599.

68 Conc. Vaticanum (Propositum, 27 dec. 1869)—Mansi, LIII, 461.

69 Conc. Vaticanum (Propositum, 19 feb. 1870)—Mansi, LIII, 473.

70 For a short historical description of each up to 1935, cf. Baucher, "Abbaye Nullius"—*Dictionnaire de Droit Canonique*. Cf. also *Annuario Pontificio* for the names of the abbots and prelates now ruling, and for other data.

Article IV. Acquisition of Exempt Territories

A. Before the Code

Out of the papal constitutions and the Rota decisions issued during the eighteenth century, there developed a definite doctrine about the mode in which prelates and abbots *nullius* acquired their territories. Questions concerning the rights and privileges of these prelates were proposed from time to time and duly settled. Nevertheless through all such questions there persisted the juridical problem of the title by which the acquisition of such an exempt territory could be sustained. This was the main question during these times, namely, whether an abbot or a prelate had really acquired diocesan jurisdiction. Once this point had been established, the problem of what rights and duties flowed therefrom was comparatively easy of solution. Here, then, will be summarized the doctrine on this point as evolved especially in the eighteenth century.

Regarding the acquisition of an abbacy *nullius*, authors propose three modes by which this can be accomplished.[71] The first mode is based on an original or native exemption. This means that a monastery had been established in a place where no diocese existed, wherefore it could claim to have been originally exempt, since there was no bishop to whom the abbey could be subject. The abbot of such a territory could then exercise quasi-diocesan jurisdiction over all the people living therein.[72] Therefore, to have acquired such an original or native exemption, it was necessary for the monastery to have been established in a place where no diocese as yet existed. Such places were referred to as *loca acephala*. Authors however did not agree on the point whether such places really ex-

[71] Bouix, *De Episcopo*, I, 535; Petra, *Commentaria ad Constitutiones Apostolicas*, ad const. IV Callisti III, sect. 1, n. 2–10; Fagnanus, *Commentaria*, in c. 3 (*nullus*), X, *de parochis et alienis parochianis*, III, 29, n. 12. The authors designate this triple mode of acquisition as *exemptio nativa, dativa, praescriptiva*.

[72] The Abbey of Fulda claimed such an original exemption though it was rejected by the Rota. Cf. *supra*, p. 17.

isted. Some held that there were no such places, but that Pope Dionysius (261–272) had divided all the territory of the known world into dioceses, thereby eliminating any possibility of the establishing of a monastery which could enjoy an originally exempt territory.[73] Other authors, on the contrary, claimed that there were places which were in no diocese. Fagnanus (1598–1678) for instance, was of the opinion that Pope Dionysius only assigned single churches to a bishop in a definite diocese, but that many territories remained outside the limits of any diocese.[74]

The former of these opinions, which insisted that there was no territory outside a diocese, based its claim on a spurious document of Pope Dionysuis.[75] But even though this particular document is spurious, Pope Dionysius is rightly credited with making a division of territory, as is evidenced by the *Liber Pontificalis.*[76] Consequently it must be admitted that there were *loca acephala.* Furthermore, there are instances on record which compel recognition of the existence of original extra-diocesan territory. The monastery of Saint Stephen in Hungary, founded by King Saint Stephen (1000–1038) had been established in a territory where no diocese existed.[77] The Council

[73] De Luca, *Theatrum Veritatis et Iustitiae, de iurisdictione,* disc. I, nn. 3–12; De Prosperis, *De Territorio Separato,* quest. VI, n. 13. Cf. also a Rota Decision of June 1, 1708, reported in De Prosperis, *op. cit.*, p. 303.

[74] "... Dionysius Papa non dioeceses divisit, sed ecclesias singulas singulis attribuit ..."—Fagnanus, *Commentaria,* in c. 3 (*nullus*), X, *de parochis et alienis parochianis,* III, 29, n. 15. Cf. also Ferraris, *Bibliotheca Canonica, Iuridica, Moralis, Theologica necnon Ascetica, Polemica, Rubristica, Historica* (9 vols., Romae, 1885–1899), s.v. "Abbas," n. 79; Thomassinus, *Vetus et Nova Ecclesiae Disciplina,* pars I, lib. III, c. XXXVI, nn. 2–7.

[75] Dionysius, epist. "*Olim,*" 9 sept. 268—Mansi, I, 1006; JE, n. † 139.

[76] "Hic [Dionysius] presbiteris ecclesias dedit et cymiteria et parrocias diocesis constituit."—Duchesne, *Le Liber Pontificalis,* I (Paris, 1886), 157. Duchesne explained that the word *parochia* meant a diocese, an episcopal territorial circumscription, or a rural parish, while the word *dioecesis* was used to designate a general territorial circumscription, and in the *Liber Pontificalis* referred to the diocese of Rome. Cf. also Baronius, *Annales* (anno 270), n. 17.

[77] Cf. *supra,* p. 11.

of Avignon in 1209 admitted that a place called Vallis de Tretis existed in no diocese.[78]

The second mode of acquiring an exempt territory is based on the grant of a special papal privilege. This privilege had to be clear and definite, segregating a territory from a diocese, or at least declaring that a territory belonged to no diocese. Privileges that exempted only monasteries or their members did not necessarily exempt the territory with its resident clergy and laity. Such exemptions were usually only of a passive character.[79]

Prescription is the third and final mode of acquiring an exempt territory with quasi-diocesan jurisdiction. This the law of the thirteenth century already admitted,[80] and it persevered throughout the seventeenth century, when a forty years' prescription with a *titulus coloratus* still sufficed to prescribe an abbacy or prelacy *nullius*.[81] In the eighteenth century, however, from the time of the conclusion of the case of Fulda,[82] a forty years' prescription no longer sufficed. Prescription now had to be of immemorial duration before it could be used to prove an acquisition of a separated territory.[83]

[78] Can. 5—Mansi, XXII, 787. For further information on the question of *loca acephala*, cf. *Glossa Ordinaria* in v. *divisimus*—c. 1, C. XIII, q. 1; c. 2, D. LXXX; c. 1, D. XCIX. Regarding clerics without a definite territory, cf. c. 1, D. XCIII; c. 18, C. XVIII, q. 2; S.R.R. *Beneventana, Iurisdictionis*, 26 nov. 1668, *coram R.P.D. Bevilaqua*—S.R.R. *Decisionum Recentiorum Partes Variae*, pars XV, dec. CCCXL, nn. 1–2.

[79] S.R.R. *Constantin., Jurisdict.*, 18 maii 1611, *coram R.P.D. Attrebaten*—S.R.R. *Dec. Recent.*, pars I (Francofurti, 1623), dec. CCCXXIV, n. 6; S.R.R. *Burgen., Jurisdictionis*, 26 iunii 1709, *coram R.P.D. Lancetta*—S.R.R. *Decisiones coram P. Lancetta* (Romae, 1731–1735), dec. DCXVIII; Benedictus XIV, const. "*Apostolicae servitutis,*" 14 martii 1743—*Bull. Ben. XIV*, I, 276; *Fontes*, n. 334.

[80] C. 15, X, *de praescriptione*, II, 26; c. 7, *de privilegiis*, V, 7, in VI°.

[81] S.R.R. *Baren., Iurisdictionis*, 16 feb .1608, *coram R.P.D. Coccino*—S.R.R. *Decisionum Recentiorum Partes Variae*, pars II, dec. CCXLIII, n. 9; S.R.R. *Constantin. Iurisdictionis*, 18 maii 1611, *coram R.P.D. Attrebaten*—S.R.R. *Dec. Recent.*, pars I dec. CCCXXIV, n. 12.

[82] Cf. *supra*, pp. 17 sqq.

[83] S.C.C., 14 ian. 1721—*Fontes*, n. 3219; S.C.C., *Parmen.*, 18 dec. 1801—*Thesaurus Resolutionum*, LXVII, 278; Barbosa, *De Officio et Potestate Episcopi* (Lugduni, 1656), pars III, alleg. CXXVII, n. 1.

From this it can be concluded that shortly before the Code there were two ways of acquiring an abbacy or prelacy *nullius*. The first was by a special privilege of the Holy See; the second by immemorial prescription. The original or native exemption was usually excluded, as is evident from the case of Fulda. Also, in prescription there was some change from the law of the earlier centuries. A prescription of forty years sufficed formerly, but in the eighteenth and nineteenth century the prescription had to be immemorial. It is further to be noted that the presumption always favored the bishop. He was always looked upon as having a fundamental right to exercise jurisdiction over every part of his diocese.[84] Consequently the burden of proof always rested on the one who claimed that he had quasi-diocesan jurisdiction, and this he had to prove either by showing a grant of a privilege from the Holy See, or by prescription which was proved to be of immemorial duration.

B. AFTER THE CODE

In the present law of the Code there is only one way in which a prelacy or an abbacy *nullius* can be acquired, and that is by a grant of the Holy See. The so-called native or original exemption, which in earlier legislation could give rise to an exempt territory with quasi-diocesan jurisdiction, is completely excluded by the Code. The Code does not explicitly exclude this native or original exemption. But according to present legislation such a mode of acquisition is impossible, for no religious institute which could become an abbacy or prelacy *nullius* can be erected without the permission either of the bishop or of the Holy See, as the case may require.[85] A non-religious or secular prelacy other than a diocese, but with quasi-diocesan jurisdiction, cannot arise from a native exemption, for such a prelacy besides being usually a consistorial benefice, which can

[84] S.R.R. *Beneventana, Iurisdictionis*, 26 nov. 1668, *coram R.P.D. Bevilaqua*—S.R.R. *Dec. Recent.*, pars XV, dec. CCCXL, nn. 1–2; S.R.R. *Burgen., Iurisdictionis*, 26 iun. 1709, *coram R.P.D. Lancetta* — S. R. R. *Decisiones coram P. Lancetta*, dec. DCXVIII.

[85] Cans. 492–498.

only be granted by the Holy See,[86] would likewise have to be erected and recognized as a prelacy *nullius*, as prescribed by canon 215, § 1.

Prescription is likewise excluded by the Code as far as the acquisition of a prelacy or an abbacy *nullius* is concerned. Canon 1509, 4° rules that the certain and definite boundaries of a province, diocese, parish, vicariate and prefecture apostolic, or of an abbacy or prelacy *nullius* cannot be the object of legal prescription. If however the boundaries are uncertain or indefinite, prescription may occur. But this presupposes that the abbacy or prelacy *nullius* has already been duly erected, and by virtue of canon 1509, 4° can only acquire more territory or lose some of its own. Recent papal documents show that the boundaries of such institutes are usually clearly defined, and hence the possibility of legal prescription concerning their proper demarcation is greatly lessened. Hence prescription as a means of acquiring an abbacy or prelacy *nullius* is totally eliminated in the Code, although there still remains the possibility of prescribing uncertain and indefinite territories.

With native or original exemption, and prescription eliminated, there remains but one means of acquiring an abbacy or prelacy *nullius*, and that is by a grant of the Holy See.

> **Canon 215, § 1: Unius supremae ecclesiasticae potestatis est provincias ecclesiasticas, dioeceses, abbatias vel praelaturas *nullius*, vicariatus apostolicos, praefecturas apostolicas erigere, aliter circumscribere, dividere, unire, supprimere.**

This canon and the following two canons speak of two kinds of territorial divisions, the major and the minor, as the authors call them. The major territorial divisions are the provinces, the dioceses and their equivalents. These major territorial divisions are made solely by the Holy See through the Sacred Consistorial Congregation if the territory is subject to the common law, or through the Sacred Congregation for the Propagation of the Faith if the territory is in missionary countries.

[86] Cans. 1411, 1°; 1414, § 1.

The minor territorial divisions, such as those of parishes, are made by the local ordinaries.

Corresponding to this there is the division of benefices into consistorial and non-consistorial.[87] A consistorial benefice is one that is usually granted through the Sacred Consistorial Congregation; all others are non-consistorial. It is to be especially noted that canon 1411, 1° uses the words "*conferri solent,*" *i.e.* the benefices do not necessarily have to be actually granted in Consistory. Formerly benefices were divided into major and minor, corresponding to the major and minor territorial divisions. Now they are called consistorial and non-consistorial, the consistorial corresponding to the major territorial divisions, or former major benefices, and the non-consistorial corresponding to the minor territorial divisions, or minor benefices.[88] As a benefice, then, an abbacy or a prelacy *nullius* will be a consistorial benefice because it is always granted by the Holy See through the Sacred Consistorial Congregation.

Two things become apparent from canon 215. In the first place, according to canon 215, § 2, the abbacy or prelacy *nullius* is placed on a par with the diocese, and the abbot or prelate *nullius* is placed on a par with the diocesan bishops in all matters, except where the nature of the situation, or the context of the law demand otherwise.[89] It can therefore be said, as a fundamental principle, that the abbot and prelate *nullius* have the rights, duties, and privileges of the diocesan bishop, except such rights and privileges as accrue to the bishop by reason of his episcopal consecration.[90] Canon 215, § 2 further establishes

[87] Can. 1411, 1°.

[88] Pistocchi, *De Re Beneficiali* (Taurini Italia: Marietti, 1928), pp. 26 and 42. Cf. also Hilling, *Das Personenrecht* (Paderborn: Schöningh, 1924), p. 86.

[89] Cans. 215, § 2; 323, § 1.

[90] "Volumus autem ut Tu (Abbas Vincentius Taylor) in tuae Abbatiae territorium et in personas ibi degentes eamden tum ordinis tum iurisdictionis exerceas potestatem, quam Episcopi in propriis dioecesibus et eorumdem iuribus fruaris ac legibus et officiis adstringaris, iis vero exceptis, ad quae exercenda character episcopalis requiritur."—Cancellaria Apostolica, 12 dec. 1924—Original document of the confirmation of the Election of Abbot Vincent Taylor, O.S.B., Belmont Abbey, Belmont, N.C.

the presumption that the abbot and prelate *nullius* have all these rights, duties, and privileges. Hence any denial of these must be definitely proved.

Secondly, by virtue of canon 215, § 1, Rome retains full control regarding the boundaries of such separated territories, just as it does regarding the territory of a diocese. The Holy See reserves for itself not only the right to establish such territories, but also the right to circumscribe, divide, unite, or suppress them.[91]

To sum up the treatise on the acquisition of an exempt territory with quasi-diocesan jurisdiction, it can be said that in very early times three modes of acquisition existed, namely, native exemption, legal prescription, and positive grant of the Holy See. Native exemption was only doubtfully recognized in the seventeenth and eighteenth century, and is now completely eliminated by the Code. Prescription underwent a gradual elimination. In the *Corpus Iuris Canonici* a prescription of forty years sufficed. The eighteenth century doctrine required immemorial prescription, while the Code excludes it altogether as a mode of acquiring an abbacy or prelacy *nullius*. Consequently, there remains but one mode of acquisition of an exempt territory ruled by an abbot or prelate *nullius*, and that is by a positive grant of the Holy See, as is apparent from canon 215, § 1.

[91] This right was already reserved to the Holy See in the earlier centuries. Cf. c. 1, D. CI; c. 48, 49, C. XVI, q. 1; Urbanus II, epist. "*Noverit tua fraternitas,*" (ad Rainoldum Remensem Archiep.),—Mansi, XX, 670. For the meaning of the terms used in canon 215, § 1, cf. cans. 1419, and 1421.

CHAPTER II

THE ACT OF FILLING THE OFFICE

ARTICLE I. INTRODUCTORY NOTE

If the canons concerning prelates or abbots *nullius* are to find application, it is necessary that the separated territory comprises at least three parishes.[1] Otherwise the territory will be governed by special laws and regulations, outlining the powers of the prelate who presides over the separated territory. These special laws will usually be contained in the document of erection. At times the Holy See, instead of issuing special laws, merely extends the Code law to such a territory in spite of the lack of the three required parishes. This was the case with the Basilian abbey of Grottaferrata, in Italy, which did not comprise three parishes. When Pope Pius XI raised that abbey to the status of an abbacy *nullius*, he simply extended to that abbot all the rights, privileges, honors and powers which the other abbots *nullius* enjoy.[2] In any event, some special provision must be made for the separated territories that do not comprise at least three parishes.

Furthermore, it must be observed here that the whole approach of this study thus far has been from the viewpoint of territory, rather than from the viewpoint of the prelate who presides over it. The essential features, a short historical synopsis, and the modes of acquisition of an exempt territory of quasi-diocesan jurisdiction have been considered. The following

[1] Can. 319, § 2.

[2] "Novae porro abbatiae *nullius* S. Mariae Cryptaeferratae, eiusque pro tempore abbatibus seu archimandritis, quamvis abbatia ipsa tribus saltem iure requisitis paroeciis careat, ex peculiari gratia, non obstante canonis 319 § 2, C.I.C. praescripto, omnia tribuimus iura, privilegia, honores et potestates, quibus ceterae abbatiae *nullius* earumque Praesules iure communi per orbem fruuntur . . ."—Pius XI, const. "*Pervetustum Cryptaeferratae Coenobium,*" 26 sept. 1937—*AAS*, XXX (1938), 185; *Periodica*, XXVII, 223.

chapters will be devoted to the personal element, *i.e.*, to the prelates who exercise ordinary jurisdiction over the separated territory. Only the abbot *nullius* will be considered.[3] It must also be remembered that the abbot *nullius* will, in the present legal status of things, at the same time be an abbot of a monastery, a major religious superior of an exempt clerical religion. Hence, besides ordinary jurisdiction over his religious subjects, he will likewise exercise ordinary jurisdiction over all the clergy and laity in the separated territory.

Article II. Appointment of Incumbents To Ecclesiastical Offices

An ecclesiastical office in the strict sense is some duty, trust or charge permanently created by divine or ecclesiastical enactment, conferred by an ecclesiastical superior according to canonical norms, and implying or entailing some participation in the ecclesiastical powers either of orders or of jurisdiction.[4] In the filling of an ecclesiastical office, three distinct acts can be discerned.[5] The first is a designation of the person who is to hold the office. The second is the actual conferring of the office by a legitimate superior. The third is the actual taking over of the office by the designated person.

It must here be mentioned that there is a distinction between an office and a benefice.[6] An office is as it were the genus, and is divided into two species, namely an office which is a benefice, and an office which is not a benefice. In the present legislation there can be no benefice which is not at the same time connected with an ecclesiastical office.[7] But ecclesiastical

[3] What will be said of the abbot *nullius* will also usually apply to the prelate *nullius, mutatis mutandis.*

[4] Can. 145, § 1.

[5] Schmalzgrueber, *Jus Ecclesiasticum Universum* (5 vols. in 12, Romae, 1843–1845), lib. III, tit. VII pr., nn. 1, 4, 16, 48; Wernz, *Ius Decretalium*, II, 388; Wernz-Vidal, *Ius Canonicum*, II, 205.

[6] Cans. 146; 1413, § 2.

[7] Can. 1409; Coronata, *Institutiones*, n. 205; Pistocchi, *De Re Beneficiali*, pp. 5 and 11.

offices which are not benefices do exist. Hence whatever the law states generically concerning offices applies specifically also to benefices, but not every specific statement of the law in relation to benefices can be predicated alike of offices in general.[8] The third act of the three mentioned above, namely the actual taking over of an office or the corporeal installation in it, is always required for the filling of a benefice.[9] But for the filling of an office this act is not always required. There is no general canon, similar to canon 1443, that prescribes corporeal installation for the filling of an ecclesiastical office that is not at the same time a benefice. Whenever such a ceremony is required, it is definitely indicated.[10] Otherwise it is not required in the filling of an office as long as the office is not also a benefice. That is why under canons 147 and 148 the Code is concerned only with the first two acts, the designation of the person, and the conferment of the office.

The first act, the designation of the person, is equivalent to what is ordinarily understood as a nomination for an office, or the choice of a candidate. In fact, even the earlier writers used the term *nominatio* as a generic term for any designation of a person for an office.[11] In the Code, however, the signification of the word *nominatio* varies,[12] but in canon 148 it signifies a right to nominate a person for an office, *i.e.*, a right to designate a candidate for an office because of a special privilege, or because of a rightful claim established in law.

The right to designate a person for an office can rise from three sources: from the right of patronage, from a special privilege or a rightful claim in law to nominate a person for an office, and from the right to elect the person to be designated for an office. According to the terminology of canon 148, a person is presented for an office if he is designated by someone

[8] Can. 1413, § 2; Coronata, *loc. cit.*

[9] Can. 1443, §§ 1 and 2.

[10] E.g., can. 353, § 1, together with can. 1412, 3°.

[11] Hergenröther, "Ueber den kirchenrechtlichen Begriff der Nomination,"—*Archiv für katholisches Kirchenrecht*, XXXIX (1878), 193 ff.

[12] Köstler, *Wörterbuch zum Codex Iuris Canonici* (München: Verlag Josef Kösel & Friedrich Pustet, 1927–1929), s.v. "nominatio."

holding the right of patronage. A nomination takes place if the person for an office is designated by someone holding a special privilege, or having a claim established in law to name the candidate. Finally, the designated person may be chosen through an election.

After the candidate has been duly designated for an office, the next act is that of the legitimate superior, or the so-called canonical conferment or institution. This is the actual bestowal of an ecclesiastical office by a legitimate superior in accordance with the norms of canon law.[13] Naturally, then, this is the most important and essential act in the filling of an ecclesiastical office. It must always be performed by a legitimate ecclesiastical superior in accordance with the norms of the law. Otherwise the conferment is totally invalid. This act bestows the office on the candidate, giving him the title to it together with all the rights, duties and obligations resulting from the office.[14]

The act of bestowal gives the incumbent in the office the full right to exercise his jurisdiction validly, unless a corporeal installation is required. This second act, or canonical conferment, can take place in several ways according to canon 148, § 1. The final result, however, will always be the same, regardless of the intermediate means employed for effecting the conferment. The legitimate superior installs the candidate in his office when the candidate has been presented or nominated. The canonical conferment takes place in the nature of a confirmation of the intermediate act when the candidate has been elected, or in the nature of an admission of the candidate to the office when the candidate had been postulated for the office.

[13] Can. 147, § 2. *Canonica provisio* and *canonica institutio* are synonymous in the Code, as is evident from canons 332, §2; 1466, §§1–2; 1467. Cf. S.C.C., *Resolutio*, 12 nov. 1921, et 10 iun. 1922—*AAS*, XIV (1922), 459.

[14] "An necessaria sit institutio praesentato, vel nominato ad beneficium, ut is occupare illud, vel administrare possit? Resp. affirmative. *Ratio est*, quia per praesentationem patroni solum consequitur jus ad rem . . . titulum vero et jus in re . . . primum acquirit per institutionem."—Schmalzgrueber, *Jus Ecclesiasticum Universum*, lib. III, tit. VII, n. 6. Cf. also cans. 176, §§ 2–3 and 177, § 4.

If the election is of such a character that it does not require any confirmation, then the canonical conferment or institution in office is had simply through the acceptance of the office on the part of the candidate elected. This latter form of institution in office obtains in the papal election. Finally, if both acts, *i.e.*, the designation of the candidate and the canonical conferment of the office are placed by the legitimate superior, then the canonical institution in the office is effected through an act of free bestowal (*libera collatio*). This, for instance, is the case in the appointment of pastors, when the bishop not only chooses the candidate, but also confers the pastoral office upon him.[15]

After the nominee has been duly instituted in his office, there remains a possible need of a third act in the assignment of the appointee to his office, and that is the actual taking over of the office by the candidate himself, or the corporeal installation.[16] The manner in which this act is to be carried out is specified in some instances; it is left in other instances to particular law or custom to determine how this is to be done. The coadjutor bishop, for instance, must show the apostolic letter of appointment to the residential bishop,[17] while those who have received offices which are also non-consistorial benefices, such as parishes, are installed according to particular law or custom, or by the very fact of a valid grant of dispensation from such a requirement.[18]

In the case of an abbot *nullius*, the candidate for the office can be designated in one of three ways:[19] by the Holy Father himself, by an election, or by someone who still possesses the right of patronage. The canonical conferment or institution in the office is always made by the Holy Father, while the corporeal installation in the office is carried out by the pres-

[15] Can. 455, § 1.

[16] "... missio in possessionem, seu institutio corporalis ..."—Can. 1443, § 2. In the assignment of an appointee to non-beneficial offices, this act is not always required.

[17] Can. 353, § 1.

[18] Can. 1444, § 1.

[19] Can. 320, § 1.

entation of the apostolic letter of appointment to the religious chapter. Hence there are three possibilities by means of which the office of an abbot *nullius* can be filled: first, through the free bestowal of the office by the Pope; secondly, through the election of the candidate together with the subsequent confirmation of the election by the Holy Father; thirdly, through the presentation of the candidate by the patron together with the subsequent institution in office by the Pope.

Perhaps the following chart will more clearly illustrate the whole process which can obtain in the filling of the office of an abbot *nullius*.

In the appointment of an abbot *nullius* (canon 320, § 1) the filling of the office connotes the placing of three distinct and separable acts.

	I		II		III
when	**the designation of the Candidate results from**	**then**	**the institution (*provisio canonica*) in the office is effected by**	**and**	**the corporeal installation (*institutio corporalis*) will be governed by**
through a rightful claim established by the law	1. an act of the proper ecclesiastical superior (the Pope)	"	1. the act of free bestowal on the part of the proper superior (the Pope)	"	Canons 322, § 1 and 334, § 3
through the enjoyment of the right of election	2. an act of canonical election (which calls for a subsequent act of confirmation)	"	2. the proper superior's (the Pope's) confirmation of the election	"	"
through the acknowledgment of the right of postulation	3. an act of postulation	"	3. the proper superior's (the Pope's) admission of the postulation	"	"
through the possession of the right of patronage	4. an act of presentation on the part of the lay patron	"	4. the proper superior's (the Pope's) institution of the presentee in office	"	"

Article III. Free Bestowal

Canon 320, § 1: Abbates vel Praelati *nullius* nominantur et instituuntur a Romano Pontifice, . . .

The first method for the filling of the office of an abbot *nullius* consists in the proper superior's act of free bestowal. Consequently, in accord with the principles of canon 148, both the nomination[20] of the candidate for the office and the canonical institution are performed by the Roman Pontiff. This will usually be done through the Sacred Consistorial Congregation, as in the case for the appointment of bishops.[21]

No one will deny that the Pope is free to choose whomever he will, and without asking for advice from anyone. Yet this would be imprudent, especially were he to nominate and canonically institute some unknown person in a country far removed from Rome. Bishops are likewise nominated by the Holy Father, and receive their canonical institution from him.[22] Yet as far as bishops are concerned, canon 330 demands that the fitness of the candidate must first be established according to the method prescribed by the Holy See. Canon 331, § 3, rules that only the Holy See can judge whether a candidate is qualified for the office of bishop. Hence the Sacred Consistorial Congregation has issued several decrees for various countries, especially for those farther removed from Rome. These decrees outline a process by which the Holy See is periodically informed of the qualities and capabilities of candidates who may in the future be appointed to the episcopal office.[23]

[20] Nomination is used in the sense of canon 148. Cf. also can. 455, § 1.

[21] Cf. can. 260, §§ 1 and 2.

[22] Cans. 329, § 2; 332, § 1.

[23] These decrees have been issued for several countries: a) United States—S.C.Consist., decr. 25 iul. 1916—*AAS*, VIII (1916), 400; b) Canada and Newfoundland—S.C.Consist., decr. 19 mart. 1919—*AAS*, XI (1919), 124; c) Scotland—S. C. Consist., decr. 20 nov. 1920—*AAS*, XIII (1921), 13; d) Brazil—S. C. Consist., decr. 19 mart. 1921—*AAS*, XIII (1921), 222; e) Mexico—S. C. Consist., decr. 30 apr. 1921—*AAS*, XIII (1921), 379; f) Poland (Latin Rite)—S. C. Consist., decr. 20 aug. 1921—*AAS*, XIII (1921), 420.

In this way the Holy See has at its disposal a list of candidates who in the eyes of the bishops of that particular country are best fitted for the office, and from this list the Holy Father makes his appointments.

All these decrees are substantially the same. The one for the United States first of all abolishes the process established at the III. Plenary Council of Baltimore (1884).[24] Then it declares that every second year after 1917, every bishop shall indicate to his metropolitan one or two priests whom he deems best fitted for the office of bishop. After Easter of each second year all the suffragan bishops of a province meet at a place designated by the archbishop. This meeting is to be altogether informal, in order to attract as little attention as possible. Here the bishops discuss the candidates, and vote on them, all according to the method outlined in the decree. They are even requested to indicate the type of diocese for which the candidate is best suited. The results of this informal meeting are sent to the Sacred Consistorial Congregation.

It is to be noted that this selection of candidates is not the equivalent of the canonical election of a bishop. It implies merely a recommendation. Although there is some balloting connected with the process, the whole object is merely to suggest to the Holy See who are the likely candidates for the episcopal office. The candidate who is suggested derives no right from this balloting, not even a *ius ad rem* such as usually attaches to a candidate's acceptance of his election for an office. In other words, the process outlined in these decrees is not a means of designating a candidate for an office, but simply a method for submitting a recommendation of someone who may later be appointed by the Holy See. By no means is the Holy See under obligation or legal constraint to appoint the candidate who has been suggested, but the Holy See frequently finds it both feasible and prudent to do so.

All these decrees were issued to contribute their aid for the full realization of the demand of canon 330 regarding the fit-

[24] *Acta et Decreta Concilii Plenarii Baltimorensis III* (1884) (Baltimorae, 1886), n. 15.

ness of candidates for the episcopacy, and hence they are primarily concerned with the episcopal office.[25] But suppose there is question of the appointment of an abbot *nullius*, would the same decrees apply?

Although Rome has made no explicit declaration on this point, the answer must be in the affirmative. Of course, if the candidate for the office of an abbot *nullius* is designated by an election, then the decrees as such would not apply, except perhaps indirectly regarding the qualities required in the candidate.[26] But in the case of an appointment by free bestowal they will apply. There is nothing in the decrees to exclude the abbot *nullius*. On the other hand there are reasons for which he must be considered as included, if he receives his office through the Pope's act of free bestowal.

In the first place, the purpose of the decrees is to suggest to the Holy See candidates who are qualified and capable of fulfilling the episcopal office. Quite naturally then, Rome would also be interested in suggestions concerning persons who are about to fill positions equivalent to the episcopal office. If Rome proceeds cautiously in the appointment of a bishop, it will proceed with equal caution in the appointment of an abbot *nullius*.

Secondly, the following arguments can be proposed to show that the decrees will apply also in the case of an abbot *nullius*.

1. The decrees are directed to the selection of candidates who are to fill the episcopal office. They are not restricted simply to those who will later be consecrated bishops. According to the principles of canon 215, § 2, together with canon 323, § 1, what is said of a bishop applies also to an abbot *nullius*, unless he is explicitly excepted, or unless the nature of the situation demands otherwise. Here, the abbot *nullius* is not

[25] The heading of these decrees is: "Circa proponendos ad episcopale munus . . ."—Cf. note 23.

[26] It must be remembered that in actual practice the abbot *nullius* is usually elected, for the religious chapters have usually been permitted to retain their right of election. But in the case of a prelate *nullius*, the office is usually filled like that of the bishop.

excluded, and the nature of the situation rather demands that he be included in these decrees.

2. Canon 320, § 2, states that the abbot *nullius* must possess the same qualities as the bishop. Hence canons 330 and 331 must likewise be applied to the abbot *nullius*. The decrees were issued, however, for the sake of safeguarding the demands of canons 330, and 331, § 3, as the means adopted by the Holy See for determining a capable candidate.

3. In the Decree for Brazil, the Sacred Consistorial Congregation explicitly declares that the prelates *nullius* must attend the informal meetings of the bishops of their provinces. At these informal meetings where the candidates are discussed, these prelates have the same rights as the rest of the members there present.[27] Now, what is said of such prelates is true of abbots *nullius*, and vice versa. The fact that they must be present at these meetings shows that they are considered on the same plane as the bishops, and if the meeting did not concern them also, why should they attend?

Consequently it must be concluded that if an abbot *nullius* would receive his office through this first method of appointment, that is, as a consequence of the free bestowal of the Roman Pontiff, then the decrees issued by the Sacred Consistorial Congregation for certain countries would apply also for the recommending of a candidate for the office of an abbot *nullius* in these same countries.

Article IV. Election and Confirmation

Canon 320, § 1: Abbates vel Praelati *nullius* nominantur et instituuntur a Romano Pontifice, salvo iure electionis . . . , si cui legitime competat; quo in casu ab eodem Romano Pontifice confirmari . . . debent.

The second mode for the filling of the office of an abbot *nullius* consists in the election of a candidate, and the subse-

[27] "Praelati vero *nullius* conventibus Episcoporum provinciae suae interesse curabunt, iisdem cum iuribus ac ceteri."—S. C. Consist., decr. 19 mart. 1921—*AAS*, XIII (1921), 223.

quent confirmation of that election by Rome. In this instance the person is designated for the office by some chapter or group that has the right to elect a candidate, while the canonical institution is again carried out by the Roman Pontiff.

Nearly all abbeys have retained the right to elect their superiors, and hence they will also elect the abbot who is to exercise the jurisdiction of an ordinary over the separated territory in which the abbey is situated.[28] This being the case, the abbot *nullius* will almost always receive his office through an election, together with the necessary subsequent confirmation, rather than through an act of free bestowal.

The election itself will be governed by the general norms of elections outlined in canons 160–178.[29] But the religious chapter will also have to be governed by its own constitutions.[30] These will be observed as long as they are not contrary to the norms of the general law of the Code.

Before proceeding to the election, all the members of the chapter must take an oath that they will elect whomever they deem most worthy before God.[31] Then they are warned against any campaigning either for themselves or for others. There is, however, one exception to the general law of elections that must be observed in the election of an abbot *nullius*.

Canon 321: Si cui collegio est ius eligendi Abbatem vel Praelatum *nullius*, ad validam electionem requiritur numerus suffragiorum absolute maior, demptis suffragiis nullis, firmo peculiari iure quod maiorem suffragiorum numerum exigat.

According to this canon an absolute majority of votes is always required for a valid election. This excludes the provision stated in canon 101, § 1, 1°, whereby a relative majority of votes

[28] Beste, *Introductio in Codicem*, p. 259; Parsons, *Canonical Elections* (The Catholic University of America Canon Law Studies, n. 118, Washington, D.C.: The Catholic University of America Press, 1939), p. 85, note 6. Cf. also *Declarationes et Statuta Congregationis Americano-Cassinensis*, nn. 85–87.

[29] For a full commentary on these canons, cf. Parsons, *op. cit.*

[30] Cans. 324; 507, § 1.

[31] Can. 506, § 1.

decides the election in the third ballot, if an absolute majority could not be attained in the first two ballots. Hence in the election of an abbot *nullius*,[32] if no one receives the specified number of votes in the third ballot, the balloting must continue until some candidate has obtained an absolute majority of votes.[33] Any particular law or religious constitution contrary to this is excluded, unless it demands a larger number of votes, for instance a two-thirds majority.

Upon conclusion of the election, the candidate who has received the absolute majority of votes is free to accept or refuse the election. If he accepts, he acquires a *ius ad rem*[34] in regard to the office, but cannot exercise any of the powers of the office before he receives the necessary confirmation of the election from the Holy See.[35] Within eight days after the candidate accepts the results of the election, he must apply for the necessary confirmation. Otherwise he loses the *ius ad rem* that accrued to him upon his acceptance.[36]

Election and the subsequent confirmation of the election, therefore, constitute the second method by which the office of an abbot *nullius* is filled. The designation of the candidate for the office takes place through the election, while the canonical institution in the office occurs through the subsequent confirmation of the election.

Article V. Postulation and Admission

As a mode of procedure which is complementary to the act of election and somewhat similar to it, there exists another means for designating the candidate for an office. This is known as postulation.[37] It is used when the candidate whom the electors wish to select is found to lack some specific require-

[32] The same requisite holds for the election of a bishop and vicar capitular. —Cans. 329, § 3; 433, § 2.

[33] Parsons, *Canonical Elections*, p. 156.

[34] Can. 176, § 2.

[35] Can. 176, § 3.

[36] Can. 177, § 1.

[37] Cans. 179–182.

ment for holding the office, as for instance when the candidate for abbot would be illegitimate. In this process of postulation, which is carried out like a canonical election, "the voters do not really **elect** the candidate; rather, by electoral petition they ask the superior to effect the appointment."[38] A candidate designated by postulation receives the canonical institution by the admission of the legitimate superior. This admission depends solely on the good will of the superior, who dispenses from the impediment that bars the postulated candidate from office. On the other hand, the confirmation of a candidate who has been elected in full compliance with canonical requirements must be granted as fulfilling a demand of justice.

A question arises whether postulation can have a place in the designation of a candidate for the office of abbot *nullius*. The general law of canon 179 allows postulation in all electoral proceedings as long as it is not specifically barred. But since the election of an abbot *nullius* is carried on by a religious chapter which at the same time elects its superior, canon 507, § 3 must also be applied. This canon excludes postulation in religious elections, except in extraordinary cases, and provided that the constitutions do not explicitly forbid postulation. If the constitutions say nothing about postulation, the presumption lies in favor of postulation,[39] but only in extraordinary cases.

In case a postulation is effected by means of a full electoral procedure, the postulation requires a two-thirds majority of votes for validity.[40] The election of an abbot *nullius* is valid only when the candidate has received an absolute majority of votes.[41] In such a case wherein there exists a twofold possibility for designating a candidate, the balloting will go on until the candidate postulated receives a two-thirds majority, or the candidate to be elected receives an absolute majority. The one who first receives the required number of votes will be the one chosen, for if the one who was elected accepts, he acquires a

[38] Parsons, *Canonical Elections*, p. 4.

[39] Beste, *Introductio in Codicem*, p. 334; Coronata, *Institutiones*, n. 252, nota 5.

[40] Can. 180, § 1.

[41] Can. 321.

ius ad rem;[42] if the one who was postulated accepts, although he acquires no right to the office, nevertheless the postulation must be sent to that superior whom the law qualifies to confirm the election if at the same time he is empowered in law to grant a dispensation from the impediment; otherwise it is to be sent to the Pope.[43]

Consequently, postulation, as a complementary act of election, is a variety of the second means by which a candidate can be designated for the office of abbot *nullius*. The canonical institution then takes place through an admission of the person postulated, which for its valid execution pertains to the Roman Pontiff.

Article VI. Presentation and Institution in Office

Can. 320, § 1: Abbates vel praelati *nullius* nominantur et instituuntur a Romano Pontifice, salvo iure . . . praesentationis, si cui legitime competat; quo in casu ab eodem Romano Pontifice . . . instituti debent.

The final method for the filling of the office of an abbot *nullius* consists in the presentation of a candidate by a patron together with the Pope's institution of that candidate in office. The candidate for the office is in the present case designated by someone who possesses the right of patronage, while the act of canonical conferment of the office or institution in the office is again effected by the Roman Pontiff.

The right of patronage itself implies the possession of a number of privileges together with certain obligations which accrue to the founders of churches, chapels or benefices.[44] Historically, the concession of this right dates back to the earliest times of the Church.[45] There existed three ways in which the

42 Can. 176, § 2.

43 Can. 181, §§ 1 and 3.

44 Can. 1448.

45 Coronata, *Institutiones*, n. 1000; Godfrey, *The Right of Patronage according to the Code of Canon Law* (The Catholic University of America Canon Law Studies, n. 21, Washington, D.C.: The Catholic University of America, 1924), p. 38; Wernz-Vidal, *Ius Canonicum*, II, 291.

right of patronage could be acquired. The first consisted in donating the land upon which the church was to be built, in actually building the church, or in endowing it. This was especially the case in relation to the proprietary churches of the middle ages, wherein, according to German law concepts, the church building as such was not a juristic personality, but merely a piece of private property owned by some landlord, to whom belonged all the rights connected with the church. The second mode of acquiring the right of patronage consisted in the grant of a special privilege to that effect. Lastly, the right of patronage could be acquired through the agency of legal prescription. The account of history is filled with the report of many abuses that arose from this right, and with the story of many struggles resulting therefrom, especially during the tenth and eleventh centuries. Pope Alexander III (1159–1181) defined the rights and obligations of those holding the right of patronage, and his legislation was substantially incorporated into the decretals of Gregory IX.[46]

The Code not only forbids any future establishment of the right of patronage, but greatly curtails the privileges of this right, and looks askance at the institute as a whole.[47] Nevertheless, the Church still admits the use of the right if its possession can be proved. Among the restricted privileges the patrons still enjoy is the right to present candidates for a vacant benefice. Consequently those who still enjoy this right in regard to an abbacy *nullius*, can present their candidate for the office to the Holy Father who will then, if the candidate is acceptable, canonically institute the candidate in the office.

These, then, are the various methods of filling the office of an abbot *nullius*, as stipulated in canon 320, § 1. Since the religious chapters have retained their right to elect their superiors, the method most frequently used in practice in appointing an abbot *nullius* is that of the candidate's election, with the confirmation of the election by the Roman Pontiff.

[46] Cc. 3–22, X, *de iure patronatus*, III, 38. Cf. also Wernz-Vidal, *Ius Canonicum*, II, 293.

[47] Cans. 1450; 1454; 1455.

Article VII. Corporeal Installation

After the abbot *nullius* has been duly designated and his canonical institution in the office has been effected by the Roman Pontiff, the third and final act for sealing his incumbency in the office must take place. This is the actual taking over of the office by the candidate, or the corporeal installation. The manner in which this corporeal installation is to be carried out is defined in canon 322, § 1.

Canon 322, § 1: Abbas vel praelatus *nullius* nequit quovis titulo sive per se sive per alios in regimen abbatiae vel praelaturae se ingerere, antequam eiusdem possessionem ceperit, ad normam can. 334, § 3.

According to this canon, an abbot *nullius* takes possession of his office in the same manner as a bishop. Accordingly the abbot must present his letter of confirmation to the religious chapter, and the secretary of the chapter or the chancellor of the separated territory will officially record the presentation of the confirmatory document among the acts to be preserved in the archives.[48] It is permissible to present the apostolic letter of confirmation through a procurator.

Before his corporeal installation in office the abbot is forbidden to take part in the actual governing of the separated territory. The question is whether the force of the word *nequit* makes the acts of jurisdiction invalid if they are executed before the corporeal installation has taken place.

Jurisdictional acts which are exercised before the canonical institution in office has been juridically effected are definitely invalid, for only through a canonical institution can an office be really conferred.[49] Similarly, jurisdictional acts which are placed after the confirmation or institution of the Pope, but before the requisite corporeal installation, are likewise invalid. In other words, *nequit* has an invalidating force in this canon. This can be deduced from the doctrine of authors, who without

[48] Cf. cans. 293, § 2; 313, § 1; 334, § 3; 353, § 1; 461.

[49] Cans. 147, § 1; 176, §§ 2 and 3.

hesitation declare that bishops, vicars and prefects apostolic, and even pastors act invalidly if they exercise their jurisdiction before the corporeal installation in office.[50] The canons dealing with the corporeal installation of residential bishops and others constitute parallel canons, from which it can be argued that if these act invalidly before corporeal installation, the abbots *nullius* likewise act invalidly under similar conditions.[51] By analogy, canon 1095, § 1 may be adduced as supporting the view that no valid acts can be placed before the necessary corporeal installation in office.

Hence it must be concluded that in canon 322, § 1, the word *nequit* connotes invalidity of action. The abbot *nullius* cannot act validly before he has shown the apostolic letter of appointment or of confirmation to the religious chapter.

The situation may frequently exist in which an elected abbot has received the confirmation from Rome, but has been prevented from presenting the letter of confirmation to the religious chapter. The law in canon 322, § 1, prescribes that a corporeal installation in office is necessary before the candidate can validly exercise his jurisdiction over the separated territory. The law however does not prescribe corporeal installation in the office of religious superior, and as a rule neither do the constitutions.[52] Through the confirmation of the election the abbot *nullius* as religious superior obtains a full right to the office, and can act validly as a religious superior,[53] unless

50 Beste, *Introductio in Codicem*, p. 267; Fanfani, *De Parocho* (Romae: Marietti, 1924), p. 91; Jone, *Gesetzbuch des kanonischen Rechtes* (3 vols., Paderborn: Ferdinand Schöningh, 1939–1941), I, 279; Vermeersch-Creusen, *Epitome*, II, n. 449; Wernz-Vidal, *Ius Canonicum*, II, 629. Toso (*Commentaria*, II, 146) explicitly states that if an abbot *nullius* exercises his quasi-diocesan jurisdiction before his corporeal installation into office, he acts invalidly.

51 Cans. 215, § 2; 323, § 1; 334, § 2.

52 *Declarationes et Statuta Congregationis Americano-Cassinensis*, n. 87. However, in the Swiss-American Congregation of Benedictines, the election of the abbot is confirmed by the abbot *praeses*, and the installation is also made immediately after the election, and presided over by the abbot *praeses* —*Declarations and Constitutions of the Swiss-American Congregation, O.S.B.* (Conception, Mo.: Conception Abbey, 1938), nn. 107, 108.

53 Can. 176, § 3; 177, § 4.

the constitutions demand an installation in office. A double jurisdiction can be discerned here, a religious jurisdiction and a quasi-diocesan jurisdiction. Consequently after the confirmation of the election, but before the corporeal installation, the abbot *nullius* whose constitutions permit it, can validly exercise his jurisdiction as a major religious superior over his monks, but cannot validly exercise his quasi-diocesan jurisdiction over his separated territory. He could, for instance, admit a novice to vows, but could not assist at a marriage.[54]

Article VIII. Profession of Faith, and Oath of Fidelity

Nothing is said about a profession of faith or an oath of fidelity in the canons treating of the abbot *nullius*. However, these acts are prescribed for the bishop by canon 332, § 2. The question now is whether they are also prescribed for the abbot *nullius*.

There can be no doubt that the abbot must make the profession of faith. Pre-Code law already required this.[55] In the Code the profession of faith is explicitly required by canon 1406, § 1, 3°. It is to be made before a delegate of the Holy See,[56] according to an approved formula. The one given at the beginning of the Code, which is based on the formula of Pius IV,[57] may be used. But at times Rome may prescribe special formulas that will be attached to the letter of confirmation.

The oath of fidelity to the Holy See must likewise be taken by the abbot *nullius*. Canon 332, § 2, requires this oath of all who are promoted to the episcopacy. The force of canon 215, § 2, also tends to bind the abbot *nullius* to this obligation.

54 Cans. 543; 1095, § 1.

55 Tamburini, *De Jure Abbatum*, tom. I, disput. VIII, quaes. III, n. 1; disput XI, quaes. II, n. 5.

56 This delegate will usually be the bishop who is to impart the abbatial blessing—Cancellaria Apostolica, 12 dec. 1924—Original document of the confirmation of the election of the Abbot of Belmont Abbey, Belmont, N.C.

57 Pius IV, const. "*Iniunctum nobis,*" 13 nov. 1564—*Fontes*, n. 108.

Two formulas are given for this oath, one for the consecration of a bishop, the other for the blessing of an abbot.[58] The former is somewhat longer, including mention of some of the duties of bishops, such as the one of promising to make the *ad limina* visit. Substantially, however, they are the same. No rule specifies which one of these the abbot *nullius* must use. Hence, unless Rome prescribes a particular formula, it seems not only appropriate but also quite relevant that the one intended for the bishop should be used.

Both the profession of faith and the oath of fidelity to the Holy See are to be taken before the abbatial blessing is received.[59]

There arises the question whether a candidate who does not perform these two acts holds the office validly. Common opinion teaches that a refusal to make the profession of faith does not invalidate one's incumbency in an office.[60] In fact, in the pre-Code law the profession of faith was made within two months after the installation in office, and a refusal to do so merely deprived the candidate of the income accruing from the office or benefice.[61] That a refusal to make the profession of faith does not invalidate one's incumbency in an office is further corroborated by canon 2403. This canon rules that

58 *Pontificale Romanum* (Mechliniae: Dessain, 1895), tit. *De consecratione electi in episcopum; De benedictione abbatis.*

59 "Volumus pariter ut, etiam ceteris impletis de iure servandis, antequam abbatialem benedictionem recipias, in manibus cuiscumque, quem malueris, catholici Antistitis, gratiam et communionem Sedis Apostolicae habentis, fidei catholicae professionem emittere ac sueta iuramenta praestare, iuxta formulas praesentibus litteris adnexas, et illas vel earum exemplaria, Tui dicti Antistitis subscriptione ac sigillo munita, ad Cancellariam Apostolicam infra sex menses transmittere omnino tenearis."—Cancellaria Apostolica, 12 dec. 1924. The original document of the confirmation of the election of Abbot Vincent Taylor, O.S.B., of Belmont Abbey *Nullius*, Belmont, N.C.

60 Schaefer, *De Religiosis*, n. 142; Goyeneche, "Consultationes,"—*Commentarium pro Religiosis et Missionariis*, XVIII (1937), 96 (hereafter abbreviated CpRM).

61 Conc. Trident., sess. XXIV, *de ref.*, c. 12; Tamburini, *De Jure Abbatum*, tom. I, disput. VIII, quaes. III, nn. 1 and 16.

anyone who refuses to make the profession of faith should first be admonished to perform the act within a definite time. If he then refuses, he may be punished by means of removal from office. Evidently until the actual removal from office he holds his office validly. The oath of fidelity is also not required for his valid incumbency in the office, for canon 332, § 2, contains no invalidating clause which points to that effect, as it would have to contain according to the principle of canon 11 if it were a requirement under pain of nullity for the incumbency. Furthermore, there is not even a specified penalty in the Code for a refusal to take the oath of fidelity. Though that is not a conclusive argument, it nevertheless indicates that the oath of fidelity is hardly necessary for the valid possession of an office, just as the act of the profession of faith is not.

Article IX. The Blessing of the Abbot

Canon 322, § 2: Abbates vel Praelati *nullius* qui ex praescripto apostolico vel ex propriae religionis constitutionibus benedici debent, intra tres menses a receptis litteris apostolicis, cessante legitimo impedimento, benedictionem ab episcopo, quem maluerint, accipiant.

Just as the bishop receives episcopal consecration after he has been appointed to his office, so also abbots *nullius* must receive the abbatial blessing. In this ceremony the abbot promises to observe the rule of his order, and to see that his monks do the same. He receives a ring to signify his spiritual marriage to his monastery.[62] Amidst the ringing of the monastery bells, the abbot is enthroned in the predominant place of his choir, and there receives the obeisance of all his monks.[63] Although the whole ceremony is somewhat similar to that of an episcopal consecration, it is entirely distinct from the latter. The bishop receives consecration, while the abbot receives only a blessing. This blessing is not a sacrament, but only a sacra-

[62] Molitor, *Religiosi Iuris Capita Selecta*, p. 442.

[63] *Pontificale Romanum*, tit. *De benedictione abbatis.*

mental, instituted by the Church. It imprints no sacramental character, and is a ritualistic solemnity arising out of monastic customs.[64]

The first part of canon 322, § 2, determines who must receive the abbatial blessing. This canon indicates only generically who these prospective recipients are, while canon 625 rules that all governing abbots of religious orders must receive the abbatial blessing. This has led Coronata to state that only those abbots and prelates *nullius* must receive the abbatial blessing who are held to do so either by a precept of the Holy See, or by their religious constitutions, and not those who are held to do so by the common law of the Code.[65]

To solve the difficulty suggested by this view, several distinctions must be made. Both abbots and prelates may be secular or religious. A secular abbot *nullius* is one whose church still retains the abbatial dignity, but who at the same time is not himself a religious.[66] Such an abbot, if he is to govern a separated territory, would have to receive the abbatial blessing only if it were prescribed by the Holy See. Again, prelates may be either religious or secular. A major superior in the Franciscan Order, for instance, is a religious prelate, while a vicar apostolic is usually a secular prelate. A secular prelate, then, like the secular abbot, will receive the abbatial[67] blessing only by a prescript of the Holy See. On the other hand, the religious prelate who presides over a separated territory must look to two possible sources whence he may be commanded to receive the

[64] Molitor, *op. cit.*, p. 429; Tamburini, *De Jure Abbatum*, tom. I, disput. XI, quaes. IV, n. 3; Pallottini, sv. "Abbas," pars II, n. 1.

[65] Coronata, *Institutiones*, n. 387. Canon 625 is the only canon in the Code that specifies who is to receive the abbatial blessing. The abbots specified in this canon Coronata excludes from the ambit of canon 322, § 2.

[66] Cf. *supra*, p. 8. See also can. 319, § 1.

[67] Canon 322, § 2 simply speaks of receiving the required blessing. But authors take it to mean the abbatial Blessing.—Blat, *Commentarium textus Codicis Iuris Canonici*, lib. II, *De Personis* (ed. altera, Romae: Del Collegio "Angelico," 1921), p. 333; Woywod, *A Practical Commentary on the Code of Canon Law* (2 vols., 5. ed. revised, New York: Joseph F. Wagner, 1939), I, 116; Wernz-Vidal, *Ius Canonicum*, II, 602.

blessing. The first is the command of Rome; the second may be the constitutions of his own religious institute.

There remain for consideration the governing abbots of religious orders, who in the present connection are regarded as being simultaneously endowed with quasi-diocesan jurisdiction. The command to receive the abbatial blessing may, in this case, come from three sources, namely, from the apostolic prescript, the religious constitutions, and finally from canon 625. If these governing abbots are commanded to receive the abbatial blessing either by an apostolic prescript, or by their religious constitutions, then there is no difficulty. They are then definitely included under the rule of canon 322, § 2. If, however, the apostolic letter of confirmation, or of appointment to the office, and the religious constitutions are silent on this point, then the question arises whether the governing abbot who simultaneously is to have also the exercise of quasi-diocesan jurisdiction, and who is to receive the abbatial blessing in virtue of the ruling of canon 625, is also included under the rule of canon 322, § 2.

Upon the answer to this question depends the interpretation of canon 2402.[68] In this latter canon it is stated that a prelate or an abbot *nullius*, who, against the ruling of canon 322, § 2, does not receive the abbatial blessing, is automatically suspended from his quasi-diocesan jurisdiction.[69] Now, if the governing abbot, whom only the common law commands to receive the blessing, is **not** included under the ruling of canon 322, § 2, then certainly he does not incur the penalty. For

[68] The answer to this question may also imply a difference in the point of time at which the governing abbot in a religious order who is also to exercise quasi-diocesan jurisdiction must have received the abbatial blessing. If he is included under the ruling of can. 322, § 1, then that point of time is reached three months after the receipt of the apostolic letter of appointment or confirmation in his office as a local ordinary. If he is not included, then that point of time is reached three months after the election—can. 625.

[69] Can. 2402 punishes the abbot *nullius* only in his capacity as abbot *nullius*. Hence an abbot *nullius* who is at the same time a major religious superior would incur the suspension only in relation to his quasi-diocesan jurisdiction; his jurisdiction as religious superior would remain intact. Cf. also can. 2219, § 1.

penalties are to be strictly interpreted,[70] and they cannot be extended from one class of persons to another class of persons, or from one case to another, even though the latter case should reflect greater demerit.[71] To impose this penalty on anyone not included under the ruling of canon 322, § 2, would be to extend the penalty to others for whom it is not intended, and hence in contravention of the principle stated in canon 2219, §3. If, on the other hand, the governing abbot is included under canon 322, § 2, then he certainly incurs the penalty.

Authors do not generally touch this point. In their commentaries on canon 322, § 2, they usually merely state the canon as it stands,[72] and refer to it again in commenting on canon 2402. Coronata[73] is the only one who makes the observation that those who must receive the abbatial blessing in view solely of the common law are not included under the ruling of canon 322, § 2. From this opinion there naturally follows the deduction that a governing abbot in a religious order, if he is also to be endowed with the exercise of jurisdiction in a territorially independent abbacy, will not incur a suspension of jurisdiction by what appears to be a violation of the law of canon 2402, for the reason that he does not fall under the ruling of canon 322, § 2, as long as he is not required either by apostolic prescript or by the constitutions of his religious order to receive the abbatial blessing.

If one judges according to the strict wording of canon 322, § 2, and assumes that the phrase "*ex praescripto apostolico*" implies a special command from Rome to receive the abbatial blessing, then Coronata's opinion is not altogether without foundation. Nevertheless, it seems that even governing abbots *nullius* who must receive the abbatial blessing solely in virtue of the rule of canon 625, should be included under canon 322, § 2. For-

[70] Cans. 19; 2219, § 1.

[71] Can. 2219, § 3.

[72] Cappello (*Summa Iuris Canonici*, I [3. ed., Romae: apud Aedes Universitatis Gregorianae, 1938], 456) and Chelodi (*Ius de Personis*, p. 325, note 3) mention canons 625, and 2402 in connection with canon 322, § 2, but make no further comment.

[73] *Institutiones*, n. 387 b. Cf. also n. 2219.

merly, as now, all permanently incumbent governing abbots had to receive the abbatial blessing. If they refused, they were suspended from office for one year.[74] The Code, of course, abrogated this penalty, and nowhere in the Code is there indicated any enacted *latae sententiae* penalty for a governing abbot who has refused to receive the abbatial blessing. But the law to receive the abbatial blessing has been retained in canon 625. This plainly indicates that the Church still wishes all governing abbots in religious orders to receive the abbatial blessing. And if the law stands thus, then the import of canon 322, § 2, seems to be ample enough to include under its ruling all governing abbots in religious orders if but simultaneously they are also abbots who enjoy a territorial rule. The meaning of canon 322, § 2, would thus be established as the following: All governing abbots of religious orders, if they also be appointed as abbots *nullius,* are under all considerations bound to receive the abbatial blessing; all religious prelates *nullius* are bound to receive the blessing when they are bidden to do so by apostolic prescript or by the constitutions of their religious institute; and secular abbots and prelates *nullius* must receive the blessing when called on to do so by apostolic prescript. According to this opinion the first mentioned of these three classes of abbots, who must receive the abbatial blessing in virtue of canon 625, even though they be not bidden to do so by apostolic prescript or by the constitutions of their order, are nevertheless included under the ruling of canon 322, § 2. Because of this they are then subject to the penalty of canon 2402 similarly as are the other two classes of abbots and prelates *nullius.*

It may be objected that, inasmuch as the governing abbot in a religious order must always receive the abbatial blessing,

[74] Benedictus XIII, const. "*Commissi nobis caelitus,*" 6 maii 1725 — "...iniungimus, praecipimus et districte mandamus omnibus et singulis abbatibus regularibus, ... qui monasteriis cuiuscumque ordinis, congregationis ac instituti de cetero praeficientur, ut, infra annum a die eorum electionis computandum, solemnem benedictionem ab episcopis, in quorum diocesibus monasteria consistunt, iuxta ritum in Pontificali Romano praescriptum omnino suscipiant ... Quod si secus fecerint, ab officio per annum sint ipso iure suspensi."—*Bull. Rom. Taur.*, XXII, 169–170; *Fontes,* n. 287.

canon 322, § 2, legislates only for the prelates *nullius*, and the secular abbots *nullius*. If this were true, then canon 322, § 2, would mark the only place in the Code where the phrase *abbas vel praelatus nullius* does not include the abbot *nullius* who at the same time is an *abbas de regimine*. Furthermore, if one considers the situation from another viewpoint, and even realizes full well the principles for the strict interpretation of penal laws,[75] it does seem very incongruous that the *abbas nullius simul et de regimine*, who has the same rights, privileges, duties and obligations as other prelates *nullius*, should be the only one who does not incur the penalty of canon 2402, simply because he is not commanded to receive the abbatial blessing by a papal prescript or constitutions, but by the common law of canon 625.[76]

The final solution of this difficulty must come from the Pontifical Commission for Interpretation. Coronata's opinion stands undefended and unsupported by other authors. It appears to be too literal in the interpretation it offers. Hence until definitely corrected, the opposite view seems preferable, *i.e.*, that the governing abbot in a religious order who also exercises quasi-diocesan jurisdiction as an ordinary, though he be commanded to receive the blessing in virtue only of canon 625, is nevertheless included under the ruling of canon 322, § 2.

As a final remark on this point, it must be noted that if an abbot *nullius* who is at the same time a major religious superior incurs the penalty of canon 2402, he is suspended only from his quasi-diocesan jurisdiction, or from the jurisdiction that accrues to him by reason of his office as abbot *nullius*. His jurisdiction as a major religious superior would remain intact. For, holding two compatible offices, two distinct jurisdictions are vested in the same person. Since canon 2402 punishes him only as an abbot *nullius*, only that jurisdiction would be suspended which flows from this office.

75 Cans. 19; 2219, §§ 1 and 3.

76 "Qui sentit onus, sentire debet commodum, et e contra."—Reg. 55, R.J., in VI°.

Regarding the time within which the blessing must be received, the law of the Code varies from the former law. Formerly the blessing had to be received within a year after the election.[77] The Code has restricted this time, ruling that the benediction of the abbot *nullius* must take place within three months after the letter of confirmation or canonical appointment has been received from the Holy See.[78] This time will be computed according to the norms of canon 34, § 3, because the starting point of the interval is implicitly expressed as coinciding with the day on which the letter of confirmation or appointment is received. Accordingly, the three months are to be understood as calendar months, and the day on which the letter is received is not counted as part of the interval. Canon 322, § 2, clearly implies that the interval is to be computed in the sense of a time which lends itself with full availability for the reception of the blessing.[79]

No special day is assigned on which the blessing is to be received.[80] The Roman Pontifical, however, rules that the blessing is to be received on a Sunday or a Feast Day.[81] Furthermore, it is proper for both the abbot who is to receive the blessing, and the bishop who is to give the blessing, to fast the day before the blessing is given.[82]

The last part of canon 322, § 2, treats of the minister of this blessing. The candidate may choose any bishop he prefers. The abbot who is simply a religious superior with no separated territory to govern, must be blessed by the bishop of the dio-

[77] Benedictus XIII, const. "*Commissi nobis caelitus*," 6 maii 1725—*Bull. Rom. Taur.*, XXII, 169; *Fontes*, n. 287.

[78] The governing abbot in a religious order who is not an abbot *nullius* must receive his abbatial blessing within three months after his election. —Can. 625.

[79] "Abbates ... *nullius* ... intra tres menses a receptis litteris apostolicis, *cessante legitimo impedimento* (Italics inserted), benedictionem ab Episcopo, quem maluerint, accipiant."—Can. 322, § 2.

[80] Bishops are to be consecrated on Sundays or on Feast Days of the Apostles.—Can. 1006, § 1.

[81] The same ruling is found in S.R.C., *Sancti Hippolyti*, 31 aug. 1867, ad IX—*ASS*, XII, 34.

[82] *Pontificale Romanum*, rubrica in tit. *De benedictione abbatis*.

cese in which his monastery is located.[83] But the abbot *nullius* is in no diocese, and hence the canon gives him the right to choose any bishop as the minister of the abbatial blessing.

The ceremony to be used is found in the Roman Pontifical.[84] Two distinct ceremonies are given there: the one for the exempt abbots who receive the blessing by papal authority, the other for non-exempt abbots who receive the blessing by episcopal authority. A distinction is also made between a mitred abbot and one who is not mitred. Since the abbot *nullius* is certainly exempt, the first ceremony will be used, and he will be blessed as a mitred abbot, since he is entitled to use the pontifical insignia.[85]

Because the abbatial blessing is reserved to the Holy See, the bishop needs a special mandate in order to bless an abbot.[86] This mandate must be asked for and received each time an abbot is to be blessed. The Benedictines, however, at the request of the Abbot Primate, Fidelis de Stotzingen, have received a special privilege from Pope Benedict XV, whereby this mandate is given to the Benedictines "*semel pro semper.*"[87] Hence a Benedictine abbot needs no longer to request this mandate. To date no special formula has been issued by Rome

[83] Can. 625. However, Benedictine abbots have received a special privilege in virtue of which they may receive their blessing from any bishop if the episcopal see happens to be vacant at the time, or if their abbey is located in a separated territory.—Benedictus XV, breve "*Pro benedictione abbatum,*" 19 iun. 1921—*AAS,* XIII (1921), 416; *Periodica,* X (1922), 339.

[84] Tamburini claims he had a manuscript of Peter the Deacon (cf. p. 10), containing the ceremony according to which the abbots of Monte Cassino were blessed. Clement VIII (1592–1605) abolished all other ceremonies except the ones approved by him.—Tamburini, *De Jure Abbatum,* tom. I, disput. XI, quaes. XIV, n. 1; Clemens VIII, breve "*Ex quo in ecclesia,*" 10 febr. 1596—*Bull. Rom. Taur.,* X, 246.

[85] Cans. 325; 337, § 2.

[86] In the Roman Pontifical, tit. *de benedictione abbatis,* at the beginning of the ceremony the bishop asks: "*Habetis mandatum apostolicum?*" Then a notary reads the apostolic mandate which gives the bishop the permission to bless the abbot.

[87] "... apostolica nostra auctoritate, praesentium vi, perpetuumque in modum, pro omnibus Ordinis Sancti Benedicti confoederati abbatibus, in posterum, extra Romanam Curiam benedicendis, ubique terrarum, generale

that is to be read in answer to the question: "*Habetis mandatum Apostolicum?*" Consequently an appropriate portion of the Brief of Benedict XV may be read, or one may simply answer: "*Habemus, vi Brevis 19 junii 1921.*"[88] It is to be noted that this is a special privilege granted to the Benedictines. Others, like the Cistercians, still have to request this special mandate each and every time their newly elected abbot is to receive the abbatial blessing.

Some authors[89] teach that this mandate is not required for the blessing of an abbot *nullius*. For a reference they cite the Brief of 1921, and give the impression that the common law no longer requires the mandate for the blessing of abbots *nullius*.[90] This however is incorrect. As far as the Code law is concerned, the mandate is still required for the blessing of any abbot, regardless of whether or not he has quasi-diocesan jurisdiction.[91] The Brief simply grants a privilege solely to the Benedictines. But in practice, by far the majority of abbots *nullius* will be Benedictines, and they can use this privilege. But it is still incorrect to make the blank statement that the mandate is no longer required for the blessing of an abbot *nullius*.

seu commune mandatum Apostolicum ad Episcopum dioecesanum respectivum directum, semel pro semper, largimur, quod ad ritualem *Pontificalis* interrogationem "habetis mandatum Apostolicum?" legi possit."—Benedictus XV, breve "*Pro benedictione abbatum,*" 19 iun. 1921—*AAS*, XIII (1921), 416; *Periodica*, X (1922), 339.

88 *Annotationes* ad Breve 19 junii 1921—*Periodica*, X (1922), 339.

89 Coronata, *Institutiones*, n. 387, b); Vermeersch-Creusen, *Epitome*, I, n. 439; Wernz-Vidal, *Ius Canonicum*, II, 602 et al.

90 "Abbates et Praelati *nullius* non indigent, sicut alii abbates, speciali S. Sedis mandato ad hanc benedictionem accipiendam." — Vermeersch-Creusen, *loc. cit.* In a footnote to this they cite *Periodica*, X (1922), 339. It seems that they misinterpret the paragraph in the *Periodica* beginning, "Quod semper valet de abbatibus *nullius* ...." But this statement simply refers to the preceding paragraph, where it is stated that by virtue of the Brief of 1921 the Benedictine abbots can, under certain conditions, receive the blessing from any bishop, like the abbot *nullius*.

91 "Codex enim, cum hac in re integre ius antiquum referat, a mandato apostolico impetrando non eximit, neque illud de iure confert episcopo dioecesano, sed enunciati mandati necessitas, sicuti antea, permanet." — Benedictus XV, breve "*Pro benedictione abbatum,*" 19 iun. 1921—*AAS*, XIII (1921), 416.

ARTICLE X. THE QUALIFICATIONS OF THE ABBOT *NULLIUS*

Canon 320, § 2: Assumendi ad abbatiam vel praelaturam *nullius* iisdem qualitatibus ornati esse debent, quas ius in Episcopis requirit.

The qualifications required for a bishop are enumerated in canon 331. The ultimate decision whether a candidate has all the necessary qualifications is rendered by the Holy See.[92] In practice, however, the Holy See determines this through the recommendations of candidates whom the bishops suggest to the Holy See. This is done according to the decrees of the Sacred Consistorial Congregation issued for that purpose.[93]

When the abbot *nullius* is a major religious superior, as will usually be the case, he must also possess the qualifications specified in canon 504, together with any further qualifications required by the particular constitutions. The two offices are compatible, and just as he assumes the duties and obligations of both, so he must also possess the qualifications required for both offices.

The first requirement is that he must be of legitimate birth, and not merely legitimated by a subsequent marriage. This is one of the exceptions to canon 1117, according to which canon those who become legitimated by a subsequent marriage are equal to the legitimate in every respect. Formerly, an illegitimate cleric could acquire no benefice which entailed the care of souls, except through a papal dispensation.[94] This disability has been abrogated, except in the cases specified by the law. Birth by a legitimate marriage is a necessary qualification that one may be either a bishop or a major superior.[95]

[92] Cans. 330; 331, § 3.

[93] Cf. *supra*, page 36. For the qualifications required by pre-Code legislation, cf. Tamburini, *De Jure Abbatum*, tom. I, disput. V, quaes. VIII–XXV.

[94] C. 18, X, *de filiis presbyterorum ordinandis vel non*, I, 17. Cf. also *glossa ordinaria* in v. *Sedis Apostolicae*, *loc. cit.*

[95] Cans. 331, §§ 1, 1°; 504.

A religious of illegitimate birth who makes solemn profession is thereby granted a status which removes the irregularity for the reception of holy orders.[96] But from this it cannot be argued that a candidate for an abbacy *nullius*, if he was freed from his irregularity by his solemn profession, does not need papal dispensation. The status produced by solemn profession does not really imply a legitimation, but simply a removal of the irregularity as far as the reception of Holy Orders is concerned. It only enables one to receive Orders, but does not legitimate him. Hence, according to canon 504, such a one, even though he be in solemn vows, still needs a dispensation to become a major religious superior.[97]

According to further requirements of canon 331, the candidate must have completed at least his thirtieth year of age. He must be ordained for five full years, be of steady habits, pious, prudent, and zealous. He must have a doctorate or a licentiate in theology or in canon law, or at least be quite learned in these sciences.[98]

Besides these, the candidate must be endowed with other qualities which will enable him to govern his separated territory efficiently. What these are may be gathered from the decree of the Sacred Consistorial Congregation.[99] Under number 11 this decree specifies that the candidate must be of good judgment and experienced in actual service. His learning is to be above the ordinary, and he must be devoted to the Holy See. His executive ability, his character, and even his health are to be taken into consideration.

[96] Can. 984, 1°.

[97] McDevitt, *Legitimacy and Legitimation* (The Catholic University of America Canon Law Studies, n. 138, Washington, D.C.: The Catholic University of America Press, 1941), p. 194.

[98] Authors even dispute whether a knowledge of canon law is more important than a knowledge of theology. According to Prümmer, common opinion holds that a knowledge of canon law is more important and necessary, because a bishop cannot administer his diocese well without this knowledge.—Prümmer, *Manuale Iuris Canonici*, p. 164.

[99] S. C. Consist., *decr.* 25 iul. 1916—*AAS*, VIII (1916), 400.

Besides all these qualities, the abbot *nullius* must possess the qualities required by canon 504. The norms expressed in this canon require that the abbot *nullius* must have completed the fortieth year of his age, and that he must have completed at least his tenth year of profession. This is computed from the time of his first or simple profession. Furthermore, should the particular constitutions of his religious order require other qualities, over and above those already enumerated in canons 331 and 504, these particular requirements must also be fulfilled.

Chapter III

THE POWERS OF ORDERS

Thus far this study has treated the acquisition of a separated territory, and the appointment to the office of an abbot *nullius*. Now the study will concern itself with the various powers and privileges which the abbot acquires upon assuming his office.

Regarding the powers of orders, only those will be considered which the abbot *nullius* acquires precisely because of his office. These are specifically enumerated in the various parts of the Code, and are, as it were, superadded to the powers of orders which he already has by reason of his priesthood.

Article I. Preliminary Note

Before proceeding in detail to the discussion of the various powers of orders which an abbot *nullius* can exercise, one may well digress a little for the sake of determining more clearly the fundamental principles on which the exercise of these powers depends.

The power of orders in general is that power which is directly concerned with the sanctification of the faithful, and is exercised in divine worship, especially in the offering of the Holy Sacrifice of the Mass, and in the administration of the sacraments and the sacramentals.[1] This power is then divided into that which is of divine origin, and that which is of ecclesiastical origin.[2] Of divine origin are all the powers of orders proceeding directly from the three orders of divine origin, namely the episcopacy, priesthood, and deaconship.[3] Such powers

[1] Beste, *Introductio in Codicem*, p. 165.

[2] Beste, *op. cit.*, p. 222; Gasparri, *De sacra ordinatione* (2 vols., Parisiis, 1893–1894), n. 1138; Vermeersch-Creusen, *Epitome*, I, n. 323; Wernz-Vidal, *Ius Canonicum*, II, 376. Maroto, "De Ecclesiae Consecratione"—*Apollinaris*, IV (1931), 248, quotes Gasparri, *De sacra ordinatione*, n. 1137, ff.

[3] Can. 108, § 3.

are, for instance, the power to offer the Holy Sacrifice of the Mass, the power to forgive sins, and the like. All the other powers of orders, which do not directly proceed from these three major orders, are of ecclesiastical origin. Hence the powers conferred through minor orders are all of ecclesiastical origin.

The powers of ecclesiastical origin are again subdivided into three types:[4]

1) Those which are attached to some rite of ordination.

2) Those which are attached to or result from some office.

3) Those which are authorized to someone by the Holy See.

The powers of orders of ecclesiastical origin may be attached by the Church to some rite of ordination. These powers are then received as a result of the ordination, as for instance the powers which an acolyte receives when he is ordained to the minor order of acolyte. It should also be noted that these powers of orders, although they are of ecclesiastical origin, may nevertheless be attached to a rite of ordination of major orders. In the latter case the powers of orders both of divine origin and of ecclesiastical origin are the result of the same rite of ordination. This happens in the case of a bishop, who as a result of his consecration receives the power to ordain to major orders, and also the power to consecrate. The former is of divine origin, the latter of ecclesiastical origin.

The powers of orders of ecclesiastical origin may be attached to some office, and result from that office. A person who then receives this office automatically receives the powers of orders attached thereto. This is the case in the office of an abbot *nullius* who with his office receives the power to consecrate chalices and portable altars.[5]

Finally, the powers of orders of ecclesiastical origin may simply be authorized to someone by the Holy See.[6]

[4] Gasparri, *loc. cit.*

[5] Cans. 294, § 2; 323, § 2.

[6] Can. 210. That this was done in the past is quite evident. Cf. c. 3, *de privilegiis*, V, 7, in VI°; Benedictus XIV, const. "*Dum apostolicae solicitudinis*," 8 mart. 1752—*Bull. Ben. XIV*, III, pars I, 451.

It now remains to see how the Church can regulate these powers. Just as the Church cannot dispense directly from a law of divine origin, so neither can the Church in anyway interfere with the powers of orders of divine origin. These are conferred automatically through an ordination to the three major orders, and are not in any way subject to increase or decrease within the control of the Church. They are perpetual, and can always be exercised validly anywhere. True, the Church may restrict the lawful use of these powers, as she does in the case of suspension, but she can never invalidate the acts proceeding from a power of orders of divine origin. Hence a suspended priest still celebrates Mass validly, though he may sin gravely by so doing.

The case however is different when there is question of the powers of orders of ecclesiastical origin. Over these the Church has complete control. She can delegate them, affix them to an office, attach them to a rite of ordination. She can furthermore declare the acts resulting from them as invalid under certain conditions, or limit them in any way she wishes.[7]

With these fundamental principles fixed well in mind, one will note that the powers of orders that an abbot *nullius* exercises are all of ecclesiastical origin, and are such as are attached to his office.[8] Hence these powers cannot be delegated by the abbot unless their delegation is specifically allowed to him.[9] Being attached to an office, these powers are automatically granted to the abbot *nullius* at the time of his corporeal installation. Furthermore, no one doubts that all the powers of orders so granted to the abbot are of ecclesiastical origin. Among these powers there is only one exception. This is the power to confirm,[10] and will be treated in the subsequent article.

[7] Gasparri, *De sacra ordinatione*, nn. 1140–1141.

[8] Cans. 294, § 2; 323, § 2; 957, §§ 1–2.

[9] Can. 210.

[10] Cappello, *De Sacramentis*, Vol. II, pars III (Romae: Marietti, apud Aedes Universitatis Gregorianae, 1935), n. 289.

Article II. Confirmation

A. The Power to Confirm

The reason for which the power to confirm is considered an exception to the general rule indicated above is to be found in the fact that this power is exercised for the conferring of a sacrament.[11] This is the opinion of many authors, and for that reason they do not consider the power to confirm as a power of orders of ecclesiastical origin. Fundamentally, however, the difficulty roots in a theological controversy, regarding which it will prove useful for the present purpose to mention the various opinions.

In the first place this exclusion must be made, namely that the sacrament of confirmation is not administered by the power of jurisdiction alone.[12] This is quite obvious, since confirmation evinces rather a power of orders than a power of jurisdiction. Furthermore, all authors require some given power of orders for the administration of confirmation.[13] The whole question, therefore, resolves itself into this: by what power of orders does a priest[14] administer the sacrament of confirmation? The answer to this question is based upon three possible assumptions concerning the nature of the requisite powers:

1) A full power of orders of divine origin,

2) An incomplete power of orders of divine origin, which

[11] Cappello, *loc. cit.*

[12] The actual delegation to confirm, according to some, is accomplished through the power of jurisdiction—Benedictus XIV, *De Synodo Dioecesana,* lib. VII, c. VIII, n. 7; Cappello, *De Sacramentis,* I, n. 205.

[13] Coleman, *The Minister of Confirmation* (The Catholic University of America Canon Law Studies, n. 125, Washington, D.C.: The Catholic University of America Press, 1941), p. 107; Connell, "The Episcopate,"—*Ecclesiastical Review,* LXXII (1925), 342, hereafter abbreviated as *ER;* Cappello, *De Sacramentis,* I, n. 204; Wernz-Vidal, *Ius Canonicum,* IV, pars I, (Romae: apud Aedes Universitatis Gregorianae, 1934), 61, note 9.

[14] An abbot *nullius* without episcopal consecration, as far as the power of orders is concerned, is merely a priest who has received these powers either through an office or by delegation. The abbatial blessing adds nothing to his powers of orders.

is completed through the faculties received from the Holy See, and

3) A power of orders, but of ecclesiastical origin.

The first assumption, namely that a priest confirms in virtue of a full power of orders of divine origin, again resolves itself into several opinions, according to the various views on the nature of the faculty which the priest must receive from the Holy See.[15]

I. The priest has a full power of orders to confirm, and the faculty granted by the Holy See really grants nothing further. This opinion however was implicitly condemned as erroneous.[16] According to this opinion, a priest could always exercise this power validly, even without any delegation from the Holy See. This opinion stands refuted by the doctrinal declarations contained in canon 782, §§ 2 and 4.

II. Another opinion holds that the full power of orders given to a priest is simply restricted by the Church, so that it cannot be validly exercised without a faculty from Rome. The proponents of this opinion must explain how the Church can interfere in the valid exercise of the power of orders of divine origin.

III. A third opinion claims that the priest receives the full power to confirm, but conditionally, depending on the faculties he must receive from Rome. One of the merits of this opinion rests in the fact that it stands supported by the doctrine of Saint Thomas.[17]

[15] All these are theological opinions that are proposed by the various theologians. Any manual of dogmatic theology will explain these opinions in more detail, and give the names of their adherents. For this dissertation they were gleaned mostly, though not altogether, from Hervé, *Manuale Theologiae Dogmaticae,* III (17. ed., Parisiis: Berche et Pagis, 1935), 613–614.

[16] Pius X, ep. "*Ex quo,*" 26 dec. 1910—*AAS,* III (1911), 119.

[17] Cf. *Commentaria in Libros Sententiarum P. Lombardi,* lib. IV, dist. 7, quaest. 3, art. 1, quaestiuncula III, solutio II, ad tertiam; Connell, "The Episcopate"—*ER,* LXXII (1925), 342; Benedictus XIV, ep. "*Ex tuis precibus,*" 16 nov. 1748—*Fontes,* n. 393.

IV. A fourth opinion proposes that the priest who confirms has the full power of orders from his ordination, but needs also jurisdiction from Rome. This opinion is not very acceptable to the authors, for they rather generally agree that jurisdiction does not enter into the question at all.[18]

These then are the four opinions in relation to the first assumption, namely, that the power to confirm derives from a full power of orders of divine origin. In each opinion the priest is presupposed to have a full power of orders of divine origin. The difference in the latter three opinions arises from the divergent explanations of how this power is curtailed by the Holy See. In answer to the question of what the priest actually receives when he receives the faculty to confirm, the proponents of these opinions cannot say that he receives a power of orders, for he already has that. He does not receive jurisdiction, because that is not needed. Perhaps he receives a certain *praelatio.*[19]

The second assumption is that the priest who has the faculty to confirm has an incomplete power of orders of divine origin, which is completed by the faculty which he receives from Rome. This opinion is acceptable to quite a number of authors. Pope Benedict XIV (1740–1758), who studied the question, is an adherent of this opinion,[20] which is based on the teachings of Saint Bellarmine.[21] This teaching of Bellarmine is confirmed by a wealth of extrinsic authority.

[18] Cf. note 13.

[19] Clarke, "The minister of the Sacrament of Confirmation," — *The Australasian Catholic Record,* I (1924), n. 2, pp. 17–20.

[20] Benedictus XIV, ep. "*Ex tuis precibus,*" 16 nov. 1748—*Fontes,* n. 393.

[21] "Respondeo: Confirmare esse actum ordinis, et eum ordinem esse etiam in presbytero, saltem inchoatum et imperfectum . . . characterem autem presbyteralem esse quidem potestatem absolutam, perfectam, et independentem, quoad sacramentum Baptismi et Eucharistiae; esse autem potestatem inchoatam, imperfectam, et dependentem a voluntate superioris, quoad Sacramentum Confirmationis. Quocirca nisi perficiatur per dispensationem superioris ea potestas, presbyter confirmando nihil ageret, at si perficiatur, iam ex ipso suo charactere confirmabit."—Bellarminus, *Opera Omnia* (8 vols. ed. nova, Neapoli, 1872), Vol. III, lib. II, *De Sacramento*

There remains yet a third and final assumption, namely, that the power to confirm is simply a power of orders of ecclesiastical origin. According to this assumption, the power to confirm may be attached to an office, or it may be simply delegated. Hence a bishop would receive this power through his episcopal consecration; an abbot *nullius* would receive the same power upon installation in his office; while other priests would receive it by delegation from the Holy See.

This third assumption is not only opposed by the formidable array of those theologians who maintain that the power to confirm is of divine origin, but it is almost completely void of any extrinsic support. Some few authors simply imply that the power to confirm is of ecclesiastical origin. They do this by including the use of the power to confirm under the restrictions of canon 210,[22] which canon quite obviously is concerned only with the power of orders of ecclesiastical origin.[23]

These, then, are the three categories into which the power to confirm may fall. Of the various opinions proposed, that of Saint Bellarmine is not only the most acceptable, but is supported by many notable theologians. The power to confirm, therefore, must be looked upon as an incomplete power of orders of divine origin, completed through the faculties received from the Holy See.

Confirmationis, c. XII, *de ministro*, p. 232; Cappello, *De Sacramentis*, I, n. 204.

[22] Augustine, *A Commentary on the New Code of Canon Law*, II, 192; Vermeersch-Creusen, *Epitome*, II, n. 323; Woywod, *A Practical Commentary on the Code of Canon Law*, I, 363; Wernz-Vidal, *Ius Canonicum*, II, 376. But in Volume IV, pars I, 61, note 9, Wernz-Vidal seem to indicate that the power to confirm is of divine origin.

[23] Toso (*Commentaria*, II, 180), in his comment on canon 210, holds the opinion that this canon is concerned only with the *exercise* of the power of orders, and not with the power itself. The same opinion is proposed in the *Jus Pontificium*, where it is stated that the power of orders is so personal that no delegation of the power is possible. Hence the whole question is about the delegation of the exercise of this power.—(Anonymous), "De delegationibus,"—*Jus Pontificium*, III (1923), 87. But canon 210 clearly speaks of the *potestas ordinis*.

B. THE ABBOT AND CONFIRMATION

Canon 782, § 3: Hac facultate [confirmandi] ipso iure gaudent, praeter S.R.E. Cardinales ad normam can. 239, § 1, n. 23, Abbas vel Praelatus *nullius*, Vicarius et Praefectus Apostolicus, qui tamen ea valide uti nequeunt, nisi intra fines sui territorii et durante munere tantum.

It is not necessary to treat here the history of this question.[24] Suffice it to say that the power to confirm has been delegated in the past by the Holy See,[25] and although in the more distant past it was controverted whether the power could be delegated by the Holy See,[26] the point is now settled. For the Code rules that this power can be delegated by the Holy See, and that the power is attached to an office, all of which is evident from canon 782, §§ 2–3. Even local ordinaries, with the permission of the Holy See, can delegate priests to confirm.[27]

The abbot *nullius* receives this power *ipso iure* with his office. This means that, when he takes possession of his office, he also receives the power to administer the sacrament of confirmation. Hence immediately after his corporeal installation in office he can validly confirm.

Two restrictions are placed on the use of this power. First, the abbot *nullius*, unlike the bishop, can validly confirm only in his own separated territory. Secondly, he can confirm validly only while he holds the office. In their own territory these abbots can confirm anyone who requests confirmation, but only under the condition specified in canon 783, § 1, *i.e.*, the proper bishop of the subject to be confirmed must not expressly forbid the administration of confirmation to his subjects by the ordi-

[24] Cf. Coleman, *The Minister of Confirmation*, pp. 22 ff.

[25] Benedictus XIV, const. "*Inter multa onera*," 24 apr. 1747—*Bull. Ben. XIV*, II, 217–218; Benedictus XIV, "*Dum Apostolicae solicitudinis*," 8 mart. 1752—*Bull. Ben. XIV*, III (pars I), 451.

[26] Glossa in c. 1, D. XCV; Barbosa, *De Officio et Potestate Episcopi*, pars II, alleg. III, n. 5; Tamburini, *De Jure Abbatum*, tom. II, disput. III, quaes. I, n. 10.

[27] Pius XI, breve "*Litteris apostolicis*," 30 apr. 1929—*AAS*, XXI (1929), 555.

nary of another diocese.[28] Outside of their territory they cannot validly confirm even their own subjects.

Regarding his obligations to administer the sacrament, the abbot *nullius* is, like the bishop, held by the requirements of canon 785. This canon rules that the bishop should administer confirmation at least once every five years. The Third Plenary Council of Baltimore, however, is more exacting in this respect. According to the fourteenth decree of this council, the bishop is to administer the sacrament of Confirmation at least once every three years.[29] This legislation is still in force in this country.[30] Since the bishop is still bound by this legislation, then it is quite certain that the abbot *nullius* is also bound to administer confirmation at least once every three years.[31] If he defaults in this respect, his metropolitan is to report the matter to Rome.[32]

The formula to be used is that given in the Roman Pontifical. The abbot, since he has the use of the pontifical insignia,[33] will carry out the ceremony just as the bishop. The simply delegated priest, however, must follow the Instruction of the Sacred Congregation of the Sacraments, on the manner in which the sacrament is to be administered by the simple priest.[34]

The Holy Oil to be used in the administration of the sacrament must always be consecrated by the bishop.[35] The abbot

[28] Coleman, *The Minister of Confirmation*, p. 120.

[29] "... Unusquisque igitur Episcopus saltem unoquoque triennio totam diocesim perlustrare teneatur, non solum ut gregem suum cognoscat ... sed etiam ut fideles tot amittendae fidei in hac regione periculis expositos Sacramento Confirmationis munire possit ..." — *Acta et Decreta Concilii Plenarii Baltimorensis III*, n. 14.

[30] Barrett, *A Comparative Study of the Councils of Baltimore and the Code of Canon Law* (The Catholic University of America Canon Law Studies, n. 83, Washington, D.C.: The Catholic University of America, 1932), p. 67; cf. also Coleman, *The Minister of Confirmation*, p. 86.

[31] Cans. 215, § 2; 323, § 1.

[32] Cans. 274, 4°; 285; 785, § 4.

[33] Can. 325.

[34] S. C. de Sacramentis, *instructio*, 20 maii 1934—*AAS*, XXVII (1935), 12 ff. This can also be found in the appendix to the Roman Ritual.

[35] Can. 781, § 1.

nullius will make arrangements either with the neighboring bishop, or some other bishop whom he can conveniently reach, to procure the Holy Oils from him.

Article III. Holy Orders

A. Historical Note

It has been the common and traditional teaching of the Church throughout the centuries that the bishop is the ordinary minister of Holy Orders. However, the power to confer minor orders, which definitely are of ecclesiastical origin, was frequently delegated, especially to abbots.[36] The first instance in history wherein an abbot was delegated to confer a minor order occurred in 787, at the II. Council of Nicaea. The Fathers of this Council ruled that the abbots could confer the minor order of lector. But the abbot could exercise this power only in his monastery over his religious subjects, provided that he himself was a priest, and had received the abbatial blessing.[37]

By custom this canon of the Council was gradually extended to all minor orders, so that in time it was understood that all abbots could by common law confer all minor orders.[38] Later on, the conditions placed on this delegated power were relaxed to some extent. Towards the close of the thirteenth century the abbot still had to be a priest, and had to receive the abbatial blessing, but he could confer minor orders also on those

[36] By an ancient custom, the chorepiscopi could confer some of the orders, even major orders at times, but usually they needed the permission of the ruling bishops. Conc. Ancyranum (314), c. XIII—Mansi, II, 518; Conc. Antiochenum (341), c. X—Mansi, II, 1311; Conc. Nicaenum II (Canones Sanctae et Universalis VII Synodi, anno 787), c. 14—Mansi, XIII, 573.

[37] Conc. Nicaenum II (Canones Sanctae et Universalis VII Synodi, anno 787), c. 14—Mansi, XIII, 573. This same canon was substantially repeated in c. 1, D. LXIX, and in c. 11, X, *de aetate et qualitate et ordine praeficiendorum*, I, 14.

[38] Ferraris, "Ordo," art. III, n. 2; Wernz-Vidal, *Ius Canonicum*, IV, pars I, 229, note 123.

over whom he had quasi-episcopal jurisdiction.[39] Finally the Council of Trent clearly defined this power.[40] It abrogated all the privileges, prescriptions, and even immemorial customs regarding this power, and ruled that no abbot, even if he possessed jurisdiction over a separated territory, could confer minor orders, except upon his own religious subjects.

Throughout the following centuries the abbot *nullius* could not by common law confer any orders on his subjects, except in so far as he was an abbot of a religious order. In this case he could confer minor orders, but only on his religious subjects, not on his secular subjects. In fact he could not even issue dimissorial letters for the seculars.[41] His secular subjects had to be ordained by the neighboring bishop, who could ordain them even without the consent, or without the dimissorial letters of the abbot *nullius.*[42]

In the Code, however, this power, for the first time, is attached to an office. This gives the abbot *nullius* the right to ordain his own secular subjects, without any dependence on the neighboring bishop.

B. TONSURE AND MINOR ORDERS

Canon 957, § 1: Vicarius ac Praefectus Apostolicus, Abbas vel Praelatus *nullius*, si charactere episcopali polleant, Episcopo diocesano aequiparantur quod pertinet ad ordinationem.

§ 2: Si episcopali charactere careant, possunt nihilominus in proprio territorio et durante tantum munere, conferre primam tonsuram et ordines minores tum propriis subditis saecularibus ad normam can. 956, tum aliis qui litteras dimissorias iure requisitas exhibeant; ordinatio extra hos fines ab eisdem peracta irrita est.

[39] C. 3, *de privilegiis*, V, 7, in VI°.

[40] Conc. Trident., sess. XXIII, *de ref.*, c. 10. Cf. also Tamburini, *De Jure Abbatum*, tom. II, disput. II, quaes. VII.

[41] Conc. Trident., sess. XXIII, *de ref.*, c. 10; Moeder, *The Proper Bishop for Ordination and Dimissorial Letters* (The Catholic University of America Canon Law Studies, n. 95, Washington, D.C.: The Catholic University of America, 1935), p. 87; Wernz-Vidal, *Ius Canonicum*, IV, pars I, 230, note 125.

[42] Gasparri, *De sacra ordinatione*, n. 936.

The power to confer tonsure and minor orders is definitely a power of orders of ecclesiastical origin,[43] and hence can be regulated by the Church in any way the Church sees fit. In this instance the power is attached to the office of abbot *nullius*. Such an abbot can validly confer tonsure and minor orders from the moment he assumes his office through the corporeal installation according to canon 322, § 1.

Canon 957 itself is quite clear, and not difficult of interpretation. The first paragraph simply states that if the abbot *nullius* has received episcopal consecration, he is equivalent to a diocesan bishop in all matters concerning ordination.

The second paragraph defines the limits within which the abbot, when he lacks episcopal consecration, can validly confer minor orders. According to these limits the abbot can exercise his power of orders only in his own territory, and only as long as he holds office. The third limitation is that he can ordain only his own secular subjects. These he must ordain according to the norms of canon 956, *i.e.*, he must be their proper ordinary.[44] Finally, he can confer tonsure and minor orders on anyone, whether secular or religious, who has the dimissorial letters from his bishop or religious superior as the case may require. All these four conditions are required for validity, as the last phrase of the canon clearly indicates.[45]

It is to be noted that canon 957, § 2, does not directly give the abbot *nullius* any right to ordain his own religious subjects, for it explicitly speaks only of his secular subjects. But since in practice such an abbot will also be a religious abbot in his own right, he can ordain his own religious subjects in virtue of canon 964, § 1, and also in view of the rule expressed

[43] Cappello, *De Sacramentis*, II, n. 289; Gasparri, *De sacra ordinatione*, n. 1138. Cf. also can. 108, § 3.

[44] For a study of the proper bishop for ordination, cf. Moeder, *The Proper Bishop for Ordination and Dimissorial Letters*, and McBride, *Incardination and Excardination of Seculars* (The Catholic University of America Canon Law Studies, n. 145, Washington, D.C.: The Catholic University of America Press, 1941), p. 302, ff.

[45] Augustine, *A Commentary on the New Code of Canon Law*, IV, 425; Moeder, *The Proper Bishop for Ordination and Dimissorial Letters*, p. 78.

in canon 959. He can ordain the other exempt religious in his territory through the dimissorial letters issued according to canon 964, 2°–3°. The non-exempt religious in his territory he can ordain without dimissorial letters, for these are governed by the canons for the ordination of seculars.[46]

Another point to be mentioned is that a governing abbot in a religious order cannot validly confer tonsure and minor orders on his professed subjects unless he is a priest, and has received the abbatial blessing.[47] These two restrictions, however, are not found in canon 957, § 2, where the law defines the power of conferring orders as possessed by an abbot *nullius*. The condition of priesthood in the abbot *nullius* is required from another source. His office, since it entails the care of souls, cannot be conferred on anyone who is not a priest.[48] But the abbatial blessing, as an essential condition for validly ordaining, is not required in the abbot *nullius*. Still, both in the governing abbot in a religious order and also in the abbot *nullius* the power to confer tonsure and minor orders is of ecclesiastical origin, and attached to the office in which they are the incumbents. But in the case of a governing abbot in a religious order, the requirement of priesthood and the abbatial blessing are added conditions upon which the valid exercise of the power depends. The abbot *nullius* holds both offices. This fact can give rise to a problem. Such an abbot, after his corporeal installation in office, can validly exercise his power of orders according to canon 957, § 2. Yet as a governing abbot in a religious order he cannot exercise this same power in behalf of his own religious subjects until he receives the abbatial blessing, as required by canon 964, 1°, for in canon 957, § 2, this power is made available for only his secular subjects, and for those who present dimissorial letters. This leads to the question whether an abbot *nullius* can validly confer minor orders upon his own professed religious subjects before he receives the abbatial benediction. In practice this will be of minor im-

[46] Can. 964, 4°.

[47] Can. 964, 1°. This was required in the old law, from the very beginning. Cf. *supra*, p. 70.

[48] Can. 154.

portance, since the abbatial blessing usually takes place before the corporeal installation.[49] Still, if for some reason or other the situation should arise, the answer to the question can be found in canon 959. This canon rules that he who can issue dimissorial letters can also ordain, provided that he has the necessary power of orders. This principle was already recognized before the Code.[50] If therefore an abbot *nullius* possesses the requirements of canon 959, he can validly ordain his professed religious subjects before he receives the abbatial blessing. That he does possess these requirements is quite evident. As a major religious superior of an exempt clerical religion, he can issue dimissorial letters by virtue of canon 964, 2°. As an abbot *nullius*, he has received the necessary power of orders with his office.[51] Both powers, therefore, are vested in the same person holding two compatible offices. Consequently according to canon 959 he could validly ordain his professed religious subjects even before he receives the abbatial blessing. After he receives the blessing, he can ordain his professed religious subjects *duplici ex titulo*, so to speak, by virtue of canon 959, and by virtue of canon 964, 1°.

C. DIMISSORIAL LETTERS

Canon 958, § 1: Litteras dimissorias pro saecularibus dare possunt, quandiu iurisdictionem in territorio retinent:

4°. Vicarius ac Praefectus Apostolicus, Abbas vel Praelatus *nullius*, licet episcopali charactere careant, etiam ad ordines maiores.

It is the wish of the Church that an abbot *nullius*, like the bishop, should ordain his own subjects.[52] But since he cannot

[49] Toso, *Commentaria*, II, 148.

[50] "Viceversa qui potest dare litteras dimissorias, potest etiam, si potestate ordinandi ceteroquin pollet, ordinare per seipsum, nam 'qui facit per alium est perinde ac si faciat per seipsum', *regula* 72 juris, in 6°; ac proinde sicut in casu quis potest ex hypothesi ordinare per alium dando dimissorias, ita poterit ordinare per seipsum."—Gasparri, *De sacra ordinatione*, n. 865; Cappello, *De Sacramentis*, II, pars III, n. 346.

[51] Can. 957, § 2.

[52] Cans. 215, § 2; 955, § 2.

confer major orders, he must through dimissorial letters have some bishop ordain his subjects, religious as well as secular. This is quite a change from pre-Code legislation. At that time the proper bishop of ordination for all the subjects of a separated territory was the neighboring bishop, *i.e.*, the bishop whose cathedral church was nearest to the abbatial or prelatical church.[53] But the Code has changed all this. The abbot *nullius* is now free to send his subjects to any bishop of the Roman rite who is in communion with the Holy See.[54] There can not be any warranted suspicion that the candidates for ordination must be sent to the neighboring bishop, as was stipulated in the Council of Trent. The idea of a neighboring bishop acting as a guardian over an adjacent separated territory has been completely abrogated by the Code.[55] Nowhere does the Code make mention of the neighboring bishop in connection with a separated territory. Rather the Code has made an abbot *nullius* equivalent to bishops.[56]

It is not necessary here to discuss the form and contents of dimissorial letters, since this has all been thoroughly treated in another dissertation.[57]

D. THE ST. OSYTH CASE

According to the principles established at the beginning of this chapter, the Holy See could never delegate an abbot to confer deaconship or priesthood. These are major orders, of divine institution, and can be conferred only by a power of orders of divine origin, which is not subject to increase or decrease within the control of the Church.

But contrary to this principle, in 1400 the Abbot of Saint Osyth in England received the power to ordain his monks to

[53] Conc. Trident., sess. XXIII, *de ref.*, c. 10; Gasparri, *De sacra ordinatione*, n. 935; Moeder, *The Proper Bishop for Ordination and Dimissorial Letters*, p. 87.

[54] Can. 961. Quite naturally, canon 965 does not apply to an abbot *nullius*.

[55] Chelodi, *Ius de Personis*, p. 325, note 4.

[56] Cans. 215, § 2; 323, § 1.

[57] Moeder, *The Proper Bishop for Ordination and Dimissorial Letters*.

the priesthood. This has given rise to a great controversy among theologians. The more common and tenable opinion is that Rome cannot delegate this power. Hence most authors are concerned with trying to explain away the fact of the actual grant of this power by the Holy See.

The whole controversy hinges on two bulls of Pope Boniface IX (1389–1404). In 1400 this Pope granted to the Abbot of St. Osyth the privilege of conferring all the orders, including deaconship and priesthood.[58] Three years later the same Pope revoked this privilege in another bull issued at the request of Robert, the Bishop of London.[59] The authenticity of these two bulls has been established beyond any and all doubt.[60]

These, then, are the facts in the case. Naturally, those who claim that the Pope can grant a simple priest the power to

[58] "Hinc est quod nos, ipsorum abbatis et Conventus in hac parte supplicationibus inclinati, ut idem abbas et successores sui imperpetuum abbates eiusdem monasterii pro tempore existentes omnibus et singulis Canonicis praesentibus et futuris professis eiusdem monasterii omnes minores necnon subdiaconatus, diaconatus, et presbyteratus ordines statutis a iure temporibus conferre libere et licite valeant . . . indulgemus."—Bonifatius IX, bulla "*Sacrae religionis,*" 1 febr. 1400—text in Egerton Beck, "Two Bulls of Boniface IX for the abbot of St. Osyth"—*The English Historical Review,* XXVI (1911), 125. Hereafter, *EHR.*

[59] "Nos super hiis, prout ex iniuncti nobis ministerii pastoralis offitio tenemur, providere volentes, huiusmodi supplicationibus inclinati, litteras et indulta huiusmodi auctoritate apostolica ex certa scientiae tenore praesentium revocamus, cessamus, et irritamus, ac nullius esse volumus roboris vel momenti, districtius inhibentes Abbati et Conventui ac successoribus praedictis ne pretextu dictarum litterarum contra revocationem nostram huiusmodi aliquid attemptare aut eisdem litteris uti quoquo modo presumant . . ."—Bonifatius IX, bulla "*Apostolicae Sedis,*" 6 febr. 1403—text in Egerton Beck, *loc. cit.*

[60] "The text of the grant to St. Osyth, which goes against this doctrine [of Santi, that only bishops can confer priesthood] is printed below, and there can be no doubt as to its authenticity; by mistake it was registered twice (in Bliss-Twemlow, *Coll. of Papal Letters,* V, 333, 334), and in addition it is recited in the rescript by which it was cancelled . . ."—Egerton Beck, "Two Bulls of Boniface IX for the abbot of St. Osyth"—*EHR,* XXVI (1911), 125; Wernz-Vidal, *Ius Canonicum,* IV, pars I, 233, note 128. The text of these two bulls is also given in Cappello, *De Sacramentis,* II, pars III, nn. 308–309.

ordain to the priesthood, point to these two documents as their argument for holding this opinion. Their opponents, on the other hand, try to explain away these two documents by attacking their authenticity, or by claiming that the abbot to whom this right was granted was presupposed to be a consecrated bishop, or by pointing out that the abbot never used the granted right, etc.[61] Much has been written on these two documents. Nevertheless, by far the more common opinion is that the Pope cannot delegate a simple priest to confer the priesthood.

Of all the explanations offered for these two documents, perhaps the best is that proposed by Wernz-Vidal.[62] They distinguish between an *ordinatio iuridica,* and *sacramentalis.* The *ordinatio iuridica* in the old law was equivalent to the dimissorial letters of today. Hence the Abbot of St. Osyth merely had the privilege of choosing any bishop to ordain his monks. Robert, the Bishop of London, complained that this militated against his ordinary jurisdiction. Hence Boniface IX revoked the privilege in 1403.

There is also a controversy as to whether the Pope can delegate a simple priest to confer deaconship. Those who claim that he can, among other arguments point to the Bull "*Exposcit*" of Pope Innocent VIII (1484-1492), of April 9, 1489, which gave the Cistercian Abbot Jean de Cirey, in the diocese of Châlons-sur-Marne, the right to ordain to deaconship. However the authenticity of this document has not been definitely established.[63] Gasparri claims that the document really exists, but that it makes no mention of deaconship.[64] Others claim that neither the original copy, nor any duplicate, nor even an

[61] For some of these explanations, cf. Cappello, *De Sacramentis,* II, pars III, n. 310. His own views are expressed in n. 311.

[62] *Ius Canonicum,* IV, pars I, 235.

[63] Cappello, *De Sacramentis,* II, pars III, n. 302. The document is partly quoted in n. 301.

[64] "... sed dum multi de bullae genuinitate dubitant, mihi, facta inspectione in archivio Vaticano, relatum est bullam quidem ibidem reperiri, sed mentionem de diaconatu in eadem deesse."—Gasparri, *De sacra ordinatione,* n. 798.

abbreviated form of this document, can be found in the Vatican archives.[65]

However, adhering to the principles set forth at the beginning of this chapter, and also to the doctrine expressed in canon 108, § 3, which states that episcopacy, priesthood, and deaconship are of divine origin, it seems that the more tenable opinion is that Rome cannot delegate simple priests to confer these major orders.

Article IV. The Power to Bless and Consecrate

A part of the special powers of orders that accrue to an abbot *nullius* is constituted by certain blessings and consecrations which the abbot may perform by reason of his office. They are enumerated in the various parts of the Code where special mention is made that such an abbot can bless or consecrate certain things.

A blessing, in general, may be defined as an ecclesiastical ceremony whereby some person or thing is either placed under the special protection of God, or destined for use in divine worship.[66] Blessings are usually divided into invocative and constitutive blessings. The former place a person or thing under the special protection of God, whereas the latter segregate a person or thing from the realm of the secular and profane, and destine them for use in divine worship.

Consecration, on the other hand, is a more solemn dedication of a person or thing for use in the divine worship. It differs from a blessing especially in the fact that an anointing with the Holy Oils takes place in consecrations.

All blessings and consecrations must be performed according to the formularies prescribed in the liturgical books. Failure to comply with this rule renders the blessing or consecration invalid.[67] These required formularies can all be found in the Roman Pontifical and the Roman Ritual.

[65] Wernz-Vidal, *Ius Canonicum,* IV, pars I, 231, note 127.
[66] Coronata, *Institutiones,* n. 722.
[67] Can. 1148, §§ 1–2.

A. GENERAL CONCESSION OF THESE POWERS

Canon 323, § 2: Si [Abbas *nullius*] charactere episcopali non sit ornatus et benedictionem, si eam recipere debet, receperit, praeter alia munera quae in can. 294, § 2 describuntur, potest quoque ecclesias et altaria immobilia consecrare.

The powers conceded by this canon, and canon 294, § 2, are powers of orders of ecclesiastical origin.[68] The interpretation of § 2 of canon 323 is not altogether clear. In view of the double condition contained therein,[69] the whole paragraph has been differently interpreted by different authors. According to Chelodi,[70] at least four interpretations are possible:

(1) The powers of canon 294, § 2, and 323, § 2, are given to all, but those who must receive the abbatial blessing can exercise the powers of both of these canons only after they have received the abbatial blessing.

(2) The powers of both canons are given to all, but those who must receive the abbatial blessing cannot exercise the powers specified in canon 323, § 2, until they have received the abbatial blessing. In other words, the prelates and abbots *nullius* enjoy the powers of both canons, but those who are held to receive the abbatial blessing cannot consecrate a church or an immovable altar until they have received the abbatial blessing.

(3) Only those who are actually blessed enjoy the powers of both canons. Those who are not blessed never enjoy them.

(4) Only those who are actually blessed enjoy the powers of canon 323, § 2. Those who are not blessed enjoy only the powers of canon 294, § 2.

[68] Gasparri, *De sacra ordinatione*, n. 1138; Maroto, "De Ecclesiae Consecratione,"—*Apollinaris*, IV (1931), 247; Cappello, "De Consecratione Ecclesiarum,"—*Periodica*, XIX (1930), 133*.

[69] "Si . . . non sit ornatus et (si) benedictionem, si eam recipere debet, receperit . . ."—Can. 323, § 2.

[70] *Ius de Personis*, p. 326, note 3.

The third and fourth possibilities can be immediately excluded, for they are not only the least probable,[71] but render the words "*si eam recipere debet*" completely useless and superfluous. It seems quite logical to suppose that, if the legislator wished to exclude the non-blessed abbots from using these powers, he would say so directly or at least implicitly. This could be done by simply omitting the words: "*si eam* [*benedictionem*] *recipere debet*," which would restrict the powers of blessing to only those who must receive the abbatial blessing. This, therefore, leaves only the first two possibilities for consideration.

Before proceeding to a solution, one must again repeat the fundamental principle, namely, that the powers to bless and consecrate are powers of orders of ecclesiastical origin, attached to an office and thereby deriving directly from the law. The Church could attach these powers to the rite of the abbatial benediction, as she does attach them to the rite of episcopal consecration. But as a matter of fact she does not affix them to the rite of the abbatial blessing. The abbatial blessing as such is a mere sacramental, and does not confer any power of orders.[72] However, the Church does at times make the valid exercise of these powers of orders depend on the abbatial blessing, thereby making the abbatial blessing a *conditio sine qua non*.[73] Therefore it is in this light that the wording of canon 323, § 2, must be interpreted.[74] For those who must receive the abbatial blessing, its reception becomes an essential condition upon which depends the valid exercise of certain powers of orders received from the office.

In a full deduction from these principles, there remains no difficulty regarding those abbots and prelates who do not have to receive the abbatial blessing.[75] Upon their installation in office such abbots and prelates can validly exercise the powers

[71] Coronata, *Institutiones*, n. 389, note 9.

[72] Molitor, *Religiosi Iuris Capita Selecta*, p. 429; Schaefer, *De Religiosis*, n. 165, *d* and *e*.

[73] E.g., in can. 964, 1°.

[74] Cf. cans. 18; 323, § 2; 964, 1°.

[75] Can. 322, § 2. Cf. *supra*, pages 49 ff.

both of canon 294, § 2, and of canon 323, § 2. Those, however, who must receive the abbatial blessing, although they have the powers of orders from the office,[76] cannot exercise some of them until they receive the abbatial blessing. And this leads to the crux of the problem, namely, whether the lack of the abbatial blessing restricts the exercise of only those powers which are mentioned in canon 323, § 2, or whether it restricts the exercise of also those powers which are listed in canon 294, § 2.

In the solution of this problem the old law will not be of much help, for the Code has changed that law completely.[77] The words in the text remain doubtful, since they can be interpreted to favor both possibilities. Consequently other means must be used to reach a solution.

The opinion that seems to be the more probable one states that the restriction applies only to the consecration of churches and immovable altars. In other words, all the abbots and prelates *nullius* have the powers of both canon 294, § 2, and canon 323, § 2, but those who must be blessed cannot exercise the powers of canon 323, § 2, until they receive the abbatial blessing. The following arguments are offered in support of this doctrine.

(1) From parallel canons, vicars and prefects apostolic, and abbots *nullius*, are all placed on an equal basis in some instances.[78] They have practically the same duties and obligations. Why then should not all the abbots *nullius*, whether they must receive the blessing or not, likewise enjoy the same powers of canon 294, § 2, without any restrictions?

[76] Coronata, *Institutiones*, n. 389, is slightly inaccurate in saying that to those who must be blessed, the *power* comes only with the abbatial blessing. This would attach the power to the rite of the abbatial benediction, rather than to the office. Coronata probably meant to say the *exercise of the power* comes from the abbatial blessing, for a few lines below he says that those who are not blessed receive this power from the office.

[77] Chelodi, *Ius de Personis*, p. 326, note 3.

[78] Cans. 215, § 2; 294, §§ 1–2; 323, §§ 1–2.

(2) In other instances the Code gives more rights and privileges to the abbot *nullius* than it gives to the vicars and prefects apostolic.[79] The Code, therefore, favors such abbots more than the vicars and prefects apostolic. To restrict the exercise of the powers mentioned in canon 294, § 2, in those abbots who must be blessed would not be in accord with this principle. But to apply that restriction only to the power of consecrating churches and immovable altars, which power is explicitly mentioned in canon 323, § 2, would imply no more than a restriction of that power which the abbots have over and above the power which they share in common with the vicars and prefects apostolic. This latter supposition is much more in accord with the Code's principle of granting greater privileges to the abbot *nullius*. Hence the invoked condition of the previous abbatial blessing will touch the exercise of only those powers which in canon 323, § 2, are listed in addition to the powers of which canon 294, § 2, makes mention.

(3) The lack of the abbatial blessing certainly restricts the free use of the powers of canon 323, § 2, for those who must receive the abbatial blessing. Since this rule is of a restrictive character, it must be strictly interpreted, and limited to as small a scope as possible.[80] If the abbatial blessing be lacking, the literal text of canon 323, § 2, can imply one of two things: (*a*) the non-exercise of all powers alike mentioned in canons 294, § 2, and 323, § 2, or (*b*) the non-exercise of only those powers which canon 323, § 2 mentions in addition to the enumeration already contained in canon 294, § 2. According to the principle of canon 19 the need of the previous abbatial blessing should then correspondingly be regarded as an essential condition merely for the exercise of the added powers mentioned in canon 323, § 2, namely, the powers which relate to the consecration of churches and of immovable altars.

(4) Finally, some prominent authors favor this opinion.[81]

[79] Cans. 323, § 2; 325.

[80] Can. 19. "Odiosa restringi, et favores convenit ampliari."—Reg. 15, R.J., in VI°.

[81] Chelodi, *Ius de Personis*, p. 326, note 3; Coronata, *Institutiones*, n. 389; Maroto, "De Ecclesiae Consecratione,"—*Apollinaris*, IV (1931), 247, note 2.

It is therefore concluded that the abbot *nullius* who must receive the abbatial blessing receives with his office all the powers mentioned in canons 294, § 2, and 323, § 2, but that he cannot exercise the powers relating to the consecration of churches and of immovable altars until he has received the abbatial blessing.

B. THE POWER TO BLESS

All acts of blessing fall into two general classes, the reserved and the non-reserved. The reserved blessings again fall into four classes, being reserved to the Holy Father, to bishops, to pastors, or to certain religious.[82]

Of the blessings reserved to the Pope, the abbot *nullius* can give the papal blessing with a plenary indulgence once a year.[83] In 1942 Pope Pius XII, on the occasion of his silver jubilee of episcopal consecration, through the Sacred Penitentiary, extended in scope the privilege of canon 914, by allowing the abbots and prelates *nullius* to give this papal blessing and the plenary indulgence twice a year, instead of only once as canon 914 states.[84] However, the abbot *nullius* can give this blessing only in his own separated territory, and on two of the more solemn days of the year. According to Vermeersch-Creusen,[85] a more solemn day is some feast day celebrated with special pomp. It may be so celebrated either because of the liturgical calendar, such as Easter, or because of some special local circumstances, as for instance when the Feast of the Sacred Heart is celebrated with special pomp in that territory. This blessing

[82] Vermeersch-Creusen, *Epitome*, II, n. 465.

[83] Can. 914.

[84] "Facultas impertiendi Benedictionem papalem cum Indulgentia plenaria, de qua in can. 914 Cod. Iur. Can., ita adaugetur, ut Episcopis ter in anno, Abbatibus autem, Praelatis *nullius*, Vicariis ac Praedectis Apostolicis bis in anno eam impertire liceat ad normam eiusdem canonis."—Sacra Paenitentiaria, decr. 20 iul. 1942—*AAS*, XXXIV (1942), 240; *The Jurist*, III (1943), 157. The decree states that this faculty has been granted *in perpetuum*.

[85] *Epitome*, I, n. 406.

could be given even on national holidays, such as the Fourth of July, or Thanksgiving, if these are celebrated with special pomp.[86]

The abbot *nullius* can also give all the blessings reserved to the bishop, except the pontifical blessing.[87]

These blessings can be given by the abbot *nullius* whether or not he has received the abbatial blessing. The lack of the abbatial blessing in those who must receive it entails a non-exercise of power in relation only to the consecration of churches and immovable altars.

C. THE POWER TO CONSECRATE

The power to consecrate is primarily an episcopal power, but also a power of orders of ecclesiastical origin, which power attaches to the very rite of episcopal consecration. Hence no one lacking episcopal consecration can validly consecrate unless he receives the power by law or thrgugh an apostolic indult.[88] In the case of the abbot *nullius* this power is attached to his office, and is thus given by the law itself to the holder of the office. However, it is a limited power, allowing him to consecrate only certain specified objects.

According to canon 323, § 2, and 294, § 2, all abbots *nullius*, even before they receive the abbatial blessing, can consecrate chalices, patens, and portable altars.[89] The formularies for these consecrations are found in the Roman Pontifical.

Over and above these powers which the abbot *nullius* has in common with the vicars and prefects apostolic, the abbot

[86] Vermeersch-Creusen, *Epitome*, *loc. cit.*

[87] Cans. 294, § 2; 323, § 2. The pontifical blessing which is prohibited is the one given with the triple sign of the cross, and according to the formula: "*Sit nomen Domini benedictum*," etc.—Beste, *Introductio in Codicem*, p. 256.

[88] Can. 1147, § 1.

[89] Cans. 323, § 2; 294, § 2; 1199, § 2.

nullius also has the power to consecrate churches and immovable altars.[90] All abbots and prelates *nullius* have this power, but those who must receive the abbatial blessing cannot validly consecrate a church or an immovable altar until they receive the abbatial blessing. Before 1931 a doubt existed as to whether such an abbot could validly consecrate a church or an immovable altar outside of his territory. Cappello held that he could not, and offered a very convincing argument from parallel canons such as 782 and 957, where it appears that the abbot's power can be exercised merely in a restricted manner, that is, solely in his own territory.[91] Cappello really anticipated the answer of the Holy See on this point. For in 1931 the Pontifical Commission for Interpretation declared that an abbot *nullius*, if he lacked episcopal consecration, could not validly consecrate a church outside of his territory, even if he had the other ordinary's permission.[92]

The intrinsic reason for the difference between the bishop's power to consecrate, which can be exercised validly anywhere, and the abbot *nullius*'s power to consecrate, which can be exercised validly only in his own territory, is very well explained by Maroto.[93] He teaches that the difference lies in the fact that the bishops have this power of orders from the rite of episcopal consecration, whereas the abbot *nullius* has the same power solely in virtue of his office. The former has never been restricted by the Church, while the latter has been restricted. The Church could restrict even the bishop's power to consecrate, since it is of ecclesiastical origin, but *de facto* she does not.

The Code does not explicitly give the abbot *nullius* the power to consecrate church bells.[94] His powers of orders are specific-

[90] Cans. 323, § 2; 1155, § 1; 1199, § 2. The formularies are contained in the Roman Pontifical.

[91] Cappello, "De Consecratione Ecclesiarum,"—*Periodica*, XIX (1930), 139* ff.

[92] "An vi canonis 323 abbas *nullius*, charactere episcopali carens, ecclesiam in alieno territorio valide consecrare possit ex eiusdem Ordinarii licentia. R: Negative."—P.C.I., 29 ian. 1931—*AAS*, XXIII (1931), 110.

[93] "De Ecclesiae Consecratione,"—*Apollinaris*, IV (1931), 247.

[94] Can. 1169, § 5.

ally enumerated in the Code, and nowhere is there a power explicitly granted to him to consecrate church bells. Even canon 1147, § 1, requires that the power to consecrate validly must be granted either by law, or by an apostolic indult.

Nevertheless, authors admit at least implicitly, as the Code also seems to do, that the abbot *nullius* has the power to consecrate bells. Usually, authors simply state that the minister of this consecration is the same as the minister of the consecration of churches.[95] Besides this, canon 1169, § 5, grants him this power implicitly. For canons 1155, § 1, 1169, § 5, and 1199, § 2, are all interrelated and call for the same minister in these consecrations. Hence, since the abbot *nullius* can consecrate churches and immovable altars in virtue of canon 323, § 2, it hardly seems to be the mind of the legislator to exclude the consecration of bells. Consequently it is concluded that canon 1169, § 5, implicitly grants the abbot *nullius* the power to consecrate church bells.

In all the consecrations, just as in confirmation, the abbot *nullius* must use Holy Oils blessed by a bishop.[96]

[95] Can. 1169, § 5; Cappello, *Summa Iuris Canonici*, II (3. ed., Romae: apud Aedes Universitatis Gregorianae, 1939), nn. 662 and 677; Coronata, *Institutiones*, n. 745; Vermeersch-Creusen, *Epitome*, II, n. 487; et alii.

[96] Cans. 294, § 2; 781, § 1. Cf. also Tamburini, *De Jure Abbatum*, tom. II, disput. III, quaes. II, n. 2.

Chapter IV

THE POWERS OF JURISDICTION

Article I. Historical Note

Prior to the advent of the Code no legislation existed whereby an abbot *nullius* was granted all the jurisdictional powers of a diocesan bishop. Rather, there are found only isolated instances wherein an abbot or other prelate could exercise some jurisdictional power which normally belongs only to a diocesan bishop. These isolated instances are, as a rule, based on some special privilege, as for instance the extraordinary privilege granted to the Abbot of Fulda, permitting him to convoke synods and to appeal directly to the Apostolic See.[1] With an increase in the grants of privileges, more and more such powers were bestowed upon these prelates. Common doctrine frequently attributed some of these powers to the prelates, even in a general manner, as for instance the power to judge,[2] the power to excommunicate,[3] and the power to alienate property.[4]

Even at the time of the Council of Trent, the abbot *nullius* had no general power to exercise a jurisdiction equivalent to that of the bishop. The churches in his territory were still subject to the visitation of the neighboring bishop as a delegate

[1] Silvester II, const. "*Pontificii nostri,*" 31 dec. 999—*Bull. Rom. Taur.*, I, 476.

[2] "Omnes praelati sunt iudices ordinarii"—*glossa* in c. 2, X, *de iudiciis*, II, 1.

[3] "Nam et inferiores praelati, ex quo curam habent, excommunicant, sive sint archidiaconi . . . sive abbates."—Hostiensis, *Commentaria in Decretalium Libros*, in v. *Praelatis*, c. 3, X, *de officio iudicis ordinarii*, I, 31.

[4] ". . . forsan intendit iste textus approbare quod recitabat Inno. *de transact. statuimus* [c. 2, X, *de transactionibus*, I, 36], ubi dicit quosdam dicere quod abbates qui habent ecclesias ad se pertinentes pleno iure, possint in illarum alienationibus auctoritatem praestare."—*glossa* in v. *proprii*, c. 1, *de rebus ecclesiae non alienandis*, III, 4, in Clem.

of the Holy See.[5] However, the Council did recognize some episcopal jurisdiction in these abbots. For it ruled that if a religious superior had episcopal jurisdiction over the pastors and parishioners of his territory, these were removed from the bishop's jurisdiction and from the bishop's visitation, unless the bishop could prove some higher jurisdiction over that territory.[6]

It was only after the Council of Trent that authors began to propound the idea that the abbot *nullius* had a jurisdictional power equivalent to that of a diocesan bishop. Some authors approached the problem by enumerating the various individual jurisdictional acts which the abbot could perform, and then by way of a corollary concluded that such abbots had the jurisdictional powers of a diocesan bishop.[7] This method of enumerating the powers first, and of then concluding that the abbot's jurisdictional powers were equivalent to those of a diocesan bishop, was at times used even by the Rota,[8] and also by the Sacred Congregation of the Council.[9] Other authors make the general statement that an abbot *nullius* has the powers of a diocesan bishop, but then carefully substantiate the individual powers which they attribute to such an abbot.[10]

Towards the close of the nineteenth century the situation became more clarified. The Holy Office declared that prelates

[5] Conc. Trident., sess. XXIV, *de ref.*, c. 9.

[6] Conc. Trident., sess. XXV, *de regularibus*, c. 11; Benedictus XIV, const. "*Firmandis*," 6 nov. 1744—*Bull. Ben. XIV*, I, 450; *Fontes*, n. 349.

[7] "Corollarie demum huiusmodi Abbates, caeterique inferiores Praelati habentes Territoria Separata regulariter possunt facere, ac explere omnia, quae sunt iurisdictionis, quae possunt Episcopi in eorum Dioecesibus . . ." —De Prosperis, *De Territorio Separato*, quaest. V, n. 53.

[8] S.R.R. *Marsicen. seu Nullius iurisdictionis*, 7 iun. 1700, *coram R.P.D. Muto*—S.R.R. *Decisiones Nuperrimae* (9 vols. in 10 [Vol. 10, Appendix], Romae, 1751–1763), tom. VI, dec. CCXL, n. 33–56.

[9] Pallottini, "Abbas," § VIII, n. 45 ff.

[10] "Circa potestatem abbatum, qui ordinarii sunt, et habent iurisdictionem quasi episcopalem . . . quoad haec quae sunt iurisdictionis posse omnia regulariter, quae episcopi in sua diocesi."—Barbosa, *Iuris Ecclesiastici Universi Libri Tres* (ed. novissima, ab auctore recognita, et erroribus ablatis, utiliter locupletata, 2 vols., Lugduni, 1650–1660), lib. I, c. XVII, n. 94. He then enumerates the individual powers in nos. 95–111, and under each gives several references to authors, or the Council of Trent.

who held jurisdiction in a separated territory were included under the term "ordinary."[11] This declaration made these prelates equivalent to diocesan bishops, though there still remained certain jurisdictional acts which could be performed only by the neighboring bishops.[12]

It seems, therefore, that before the advent of the Code the argumentation proceeded from the particular powers to the general. In other words, the presumption was in favor of the abbot's not having such powers, unless these could be individually proved. The Code, however, gives them a general jurisdiction equivalent to that of a diocesan bishop.

ARTICLE II. JURISDICTION

Canon 323, § 1: Abbas vel Praelatus *nullius* easdem potestates ordinarias easdemque obligationes cum iisdem sanctionibus habet, quae competunt Episcopis residentialibus in propria dioecesi.

The powers of orders that an abbot *nullius* acquires are definitely outlined under separate canons in the Code. But the powers of jurisdiction are all provided for in the first paragraph of canon 323. This paragraph surpasses anything ever enacted in pre-Code legislation regarding these prelates. Formerly it was frequently argued that, because the abbot *nullius* could perform certain acts that normally only the bishop could perform, he was considered to have a quasi-episcopal jurisdiction. The Code has just reversed this process. Now it must be argued that, because the abbot *nullius* has quasi-diocesan jurisdiction, he can perform all the jurisdictional acts of a diocesan bishop. In other words, the presumption now lies in favor of the abbot *nullius*'s possessing all the jurisdictional powers of the diocesan ordinary. The contrary must be proved to overcome this presumption in a particular case. Furthermore, the canon makes

[11] S.C.S. Off., *litt. encycl.*, 20 febr. 1888 — *Fontes*, n. 1109; *ASS*, XX (1887–1888), 543–544.

[12] E.g., visitation of churches—Conc. Trident., sess. XXIV, *de ref.*, c. 9.

no exception. The fullest jurisdictional power of a residential bishop is hereby conferred upon the abbot who rules over a separated territory. His power is completely and in every respect equivalent to that of a diocesan bishop.[13] Hence it is hard to see why some doubt whether such an abbot can convoke a synod.[14] Rather, it should be said that he must convoke a synod once every ten years.[15]

In consequence, the abbot *nullius* governs his separated territory in matters spiritual as well as temporal. He holds the legislative, judicial, and coercive powers, which he is to use according to the norms of canon law.[16] These are his powers in general. To determine these powers specifically, as they are contained in the various canons, the following principles must be remembered:

1) The presumption is that an abbot *nullius* has the same jurisdictional powers as the diocesan bishop. If the contrary is to obtain, then it must be proved in particular instances.[17]

2) The abbot who governs an independent territory is included under the term "bishop," unless he is excepted by the canon, or unless the nature of the matter at hand demands his exclusion. He is also included under the term "local ordinary."[18]

3) As a major religious superior of an exempt clerical religion he is also included under the term "ordinary."[19]

These principles enable one to see just what canons apply to the abbot *nullius*.

[13] Toso, *Commentaria*, II, 147.

[14] Baucher, "Abbaye Nullius"—*Dictionnaire de Droit Canonique*.

[15] Cans. 323, § 1; 215, § 2; 356, § 1.

[16] Can. 335, § 1.

[17] Can. 323, § 1.

[18] Cans. 198, § 2; 215, § 2. Cf. *supra*, p. XV.

[19] Can. 198, § 1. Cf. Keene, *Religious Ordinaries and Canon 198* (The Catholic University of America Canon Law Studies, n. 135, Washington, D.C.: The Catholic University of America Press, 1942), pp. 9–14.

Formerly the authors were wont to consider the question whether the power of jurisdiction which the abbot exercised was of divine or ecclesiastical origin.[20] The Code however has settled this question. It definitely states that only the papacy an the episcopacy are of divine origin. All other jurisdictions are of ecclesiastical origin.[21]

Another question that may arise is whether the abbot's power is proper or vicarious. Hilling[22] maintains that the abbot *nullius* possesses ordinary vicarious jurisdiction. Other authors[23] teach that the jurisdiction of the abbot *nullius* is an ordinary proper jurisdiction. The answer to the question lies in a clear concept of what is meant by the words "proper" and "vicarious."

The Code does not define these terms. But authors base the distinction into proper and vicarious jurisdiction on the manner in which a person exercises his ordinary jurisdiction. If he exercises an ordinary jurisdiction in his own name, as being directly and principally endowed with such power, then such a person is said to have an ordinary *proper* jurisdiction. If on the other hand a person is endowed with an ordinary jurisdiction which he exercises in the name of another, as a vicar of someone, then that person's jurisdiction is ordinary, but *vicarious*.[24] The classical example of an ordinary vicarious power is the power of the vicar general of a diocese.

[20] Tamburini, *De Jure Abbatum*, tom. II, disput. I, quaest. III.

[21] Can. 108, § 3.

[22] *Das Personenrecht des Codex Iuris Canonici* (Paderborn: Schöningh 1924), § 50.

[23] Ojetti, *Synopsis Rerum Moralium et Iuris Pontificii* (Romae, 1899), sub v. "Praelatus"; Oesterle, *Praelectiones Iuris Canonici* (Manuscripti instar, Romae: Collegio S. Anselmi, 1931), p. 163; Toso, *Commentaria*, II, 144.

[24] "Propria iurisdictio est quae non solum ex officio habetur, sed etiam nomine proprio exercetur, idest non vices ac partes alterius gerendo; vicaria autem est quae ex officio quidem habetur at alieno nomine exercetur, quia per se ad alium, tamquam principalem, spectaret, cuius veluti substitutus et accessoria persona habetur ille qui vicarius existit.

"Tria igitur concurrunt ad constituendam potestatem iurisdictionis propriam: *a*) quod sit officio adnexa, *b*) quod adnexio facta sit ex iure, *c*) quod

All jurisdictional powers in the church, except the papacy and the episcopacy, are of ecclesiastical origin,[25] and all jurisdictional powers of ecclesiastical origin derive from, and participate in either the papacy or episcopacy.[26] Yet, since the basis for the distinction of proper and vicarious ordinary jurisdiction rests on the manner in which this ordinary jurisdiction is exercised, it is quite possible to have an ordinary proper jurisdiction that is derived from some higher jurisdiction. Some of this higher jurisdiction can be directly and principally granted to an individual, and exercised in this individual's own name. In this case he will not be a mere agent or vicar, but will rule as directly endowed with jurisdiction, though not independent of the higher authority that endowed him with this ordinary proper jurisdiction. Thus pastors, for instance, receive their power from the law, and rule their parishes not as the bishops' agents or vicars, but in their own name,[27] though not as completely independent from the bishop. They participate in the jurisdiction of the bishop,[28] but still have an ordinary proper (not vicarious) jurisdiction in the internal forum.

The abbot *nullius* participates in the jurisdiction of the papacy, and exercises a jurisdiction which finds its source in the jurisdiction of the papacy.[29] If the abbot *nullius* exercises his jurisdiction as an agent or vicar of the Holy See, and in the name of the Holy See, his jurisdiction is ordinary, but vicarious. If, however, he exercises his jurisdiction in his own name,

nomine proprio exerceri possit, tamquam a persona directe et principaliter tali potestate praedita."—Ottaviani, *Institutiones Iuris Publici Ecclesiastici* (2 vols., ed. altera emendata et aucta, Romae: Typis Polyglottis Vaticanis, vol. I, 1935, vol. II, 1936), n. 121. Cf. also Wernz-Vidal, *Ius Canonicum,* II, 359; Vermeersch-Creusen, *Epitome,* I, n. 315, et alii.

25 Can. 108, § 3.

26 *Codex Iuris Canonici,* lib. II, tit. VII–VIII. Cf. also Wernz-Vidal, *Ius Canonicum,* II, 390.

27 Coronata, *Institutiones,* n. 466; Munerati, *Iuris Ecclesiastici Publici et Privati Elementa* (4. ed., Romae: ex Schola Typographica Salesiana, 1926), p. 187; Wernz-Vidal, *Ius Canonicum,* II, 782–783.

28 They are treated under title VIII of book II of the Code.

29 *Codex Iuris Canonici,* lib. II, tit. VII; Wernz-Vidal, *Ius Canonicum,* II, 390.

he possesses an ordinary proper jurisdiction. The Code seems to indicate that the abbot *nullius* has an ordinary proper jurisdiction.

1) Whenever the Code grants an ordinary vicarious jurisdictional power, there is always some hint of its being exercised in the name of another. This is usually done through such phrases as, "unless the Holy See or the bishop reserves something for himself," "he has the rights and duties as outlined in the apostolic letter," and so on.[30] But in the canons on the abbot *nullius* no such phrase can be found.

2) The abbot *nullius* can appoint a vicar general, who will exercise an ordinary *vicarious* jurisdiction in the separated territory.[31] The vicar general will then act as the vicar of the abbot *nullius*. The abbot *nullius*, therefore, must have ordinary *proper* jurisdiction, for one would hardly expect to have a vicarious power as vicarious to another vicarious power.

All this points to the fact that the more tenable opinion is that of the authors who maintain that the abbot *nullius* has an ordinary proper jurisdiction.[32]

Article III. Duties and Obligations

The duties and obligations of an abbot *nullius* are indicated in the same canon, 323, § 1, where it is stated that his duties and obligations are the same as those of the diocesan bishop. Hence it was thought advisable to treat them under the chapter on jurisdiction.

A. General Duties and Obligations

Regarding the duties and obligations of the abbot *nullius*, the situation is the same as regarding jurisdiction. Before the advent of the Code no general legislation was to be found

[30] Cans. 294, § 1; 314; 351, § 1; 368, § 1; 1573, §§ 1–2.
[31] Can. 323, § 3.
[32] Cf. note 23.

which imposed the diocesan bishop's duties upon the abbot *nullius*. But there are traceable specific instances wherein certain obligations were imposed on these abbots. For instance, Pope Benedict XIV imposed upon them the obligation of making the *ad limina* visit,[33] and Pope Leo XIII ruled that they were held to say the *missa pro populo*.[34] But canon 323, § 1, places upon the abbot *nullius* all the obligations of the diocesan bishop. Just as there is an equal sharing of jurisdiction, so there is a uniform subjection to obligations. The presumption again is the same, namely, that every single duty of the bishop is also incumbent on the abbot *nullius*. Like the bishop, he is the ordinary and immediate pastor of all his subjects.[35] He has the duty of governing his territory according to the norms of law,[36] and must watch over the discipline of his territory, especially concerning the administration of the sacraments and sacramentals, the divine worship, preaching, indulgences, and the proper fulfilling of last wills and testaments. He must also safeguard the faith and morals of his subjects, and take care of the education of youth.[37]

B. DUTIES IN REGARD TO COUNCILS

Although the duties and obligations of the abbot *nullius* are regulated in one general canon, canon 323, § 1, there are nevertheless other canons which specifically mention such abbots, and impose obligations on them. Such are the canons which treat of the holding of councils, and which require the abbot *nullius* to be personally present.

First in line there is question of the oecumenical council. The abbot *nullius* must personally attend such a council, unless he can prove himself legitimately impeded, in which case he can be represented by a procurator.[38]

[33] Benedictus XIV, const. "*Quod sancta*," 23 nov. 1740—*Bull. Ben. XIV*, I, 15; *Fontes*, n. 303.

[34] Leo XIII, litt. ap. "*In suprema*," 10 iun. 1882—*Fontes*, n. 585.

[35] Cans. 323, § 1; 334, § 1.

[36] Can. 335, § 1.

[37] Can. 336, § 2.

[38] Cans. 223, § 1, 3°; 224, § 1.

Next in line is the plenary council. This the abbot *nullius* must likewise attend personally.[39] If however he has a legitimate excuse, he may send a procurator to represent him.[40] Both at the oecumenical and also at the plenary council the abbot *nullius* has a definitive vote.[41]

Regarding the provincial council, the abbot *nullius* must attend those councils which his metropolitan convokes. Hence the first requisite is that he belong to some metropolitan see. If he does not as yet belong to any, canon 285 rules that he must, once and for all, choose a metropolitan whose provincial councils he must attend. His choice must be approved by Rome, and he is held to choose the neighboring metropolitan. Just who the neighboring metropolitan may be is not specified in the canon. But in the past it has been indicated that the neighboring bishop or archbishop was always he whose cathedral church was nearest to the abbatial church.[42] This would establish a norm for determining the neighboring archbishop. Yet this cannot be taken too literally, so that the distance from one church to the other be measured mile by mile in a straight line. It seems that traveling facilities must be taken into consideration.[43] Quite often a church farther removed is easier of access in view of the more expeditious means of transportation. In any event, Rome will give the final decision, for this choice must be approved by Rome, after which it can no longer be changed.[44]

The abbot *nullius*, then, must attend the provincial councils of this metropolitan see of his choice. He has the right of a definitive vote at these councils, and may send a procurator if he is hindered from attending personally.[45] Besides this duty

[39] Can. 282, § 1.

[40] Can. 287, § 1.

[41] Can. 223, § 1; 282, § 1.

[42] Augustine, *A Commentary on the New Code of Canon Law*, II, 301; Gasparri, *De sacra ordinatione*, n. 935.

[43] Gasparri, *loc. cit.*

[44] Augustine, *A Commentary on the New Code of Canon Law*, II, 301.

[45] Cans. 286, § 1; 287, § 1.

of attending the provincial council, the choice of a metropolitan will have the following juridical results:

1) The abbot *nullius* becomes a suffragan of the metropolitan of his choice.

2) He must observe the decrees of the provincial council, and see to it that they are observed in his territory.[46] He can not dispense from either these decrees or those of a plenary council, except in a particular case, and for a just cause.[47]

3) He becomes subject to the metropolitan according to the norms of canon 274.

4) Every five years he should be called, and he must correspondingly attend the meetings of the bishops to discuss the affairs of their dioceses, as called for by canon 292, §§ 1–2.

5) If the abbot should incur an excommunication, a suspension, or an interdict, the metropolitan whom he has chosen will inform the Holy See about the situation.[48]

6) If upon vacancy the religious chapter should fail to select a vicar or administrator within eight days, and the religious constitutions do not provide for the situation, the metropolitan has the duty to interfere according to the norms of canon 432, §3.

7) Finally, the court of the chosen metropolitan becomes the abbot *nullius*'s court of second instance.[49]

Article IV. Indulgences

As part of the abbot's power of jurisdiction, there exists the special power to grant indulgences under certain conditions.

An indulgence can be defined as the remission of the temporal punishment due to sins already forgiven.[50] Indulgences

[46] Can. 285.
[47] Can. 291, § 2.
[48] Can. 429, § 5.
[49] Cans. 274, 7°; 1594, § 1.
[50] Can. 911.

can be granted only by the Holy Father, or by those to whom the law expressly gives the power to grant them.[51] Consequently even cardinals and bishops can grant indulgences only when a specific canon definitely gives them permission to do so.[52]

The granting of an indulgence pertains to the power of jurisdiction rather than to the power of orders.[53] Hence, according to canon 323, § 1, the abbot *nullius* would be enabled to grant the same indulgences that a bishop can grant. But the positive law of canon 912 contravenes the presumption established by canon 323, § 1. Canon 912 rules that only those can grant indulgences who are expressly permitted to do so by law. Consequently the specific determination of the abbot *nullius*'s power to grant indulgences must be sought in the particular canons which permit him to grant certain indulgences.[54]

The first of these canons is canon 294, § 2 (together with canon 323, § 1). This canon gives the abbot *nullius* the right to grant an indulgence of fifty days. However the Sacred Penitentiary, in a special decree of 1942, gave such abbots the power to grant an indulgence of 100 days.[55] This indulgence can be granted only in the abbot *nullius*'s own separated territory, and as long as he holds office. Furthermore, he cannot grant this indulgence before his installation in office.[56] The in-

[51] Can. 912.

[52] Cans. 239, § 1, 24°; 349, § 2, 2°; 274, 2°.

[53] Fanfani, *De Indulgentiis* (ed. altera, Romae: Marietti, 1926), n. 5; Hagedorn, *General Legislation on Indulgences* (The Catholic University of America Canon Law Studies, n. 22, Washington, D.C.: The Catholic University of America, 1924), p. 75; Vermeersch, "Annotationes,"—*Periodica*, XX (1931), 419. Cf. also cans. 912; 913.

[54] Actually, the abbot *nullius* can grant almost the same indulgences as the bishop, but not in view of any authorization contained in canon 323, §1. He is expressly permitted to do so by certain canons. Cf. cans. 294, § 2; 323, § 2; 349, § 2, 2°; 914; 916; 1166, § 3.

[55] "Itemque facultas Indulgentias concedendi, Abbatibus ac Praelatis *nullius* per can. 323 data, ... sic augetur, ut iisdem liceat *Indulgentiam centum dierum* concedere."—Sacra Poenitentiaria, decr. 20 iul. 1942—*AAS*, XXXIV (1942), 240; *The Jurist*, III (1943), 157. This grant was given as a permanent grant.

[56] Can. 322, § 1; 349, § 2, 2°.

dulgence is applicable only to the living, and he cannot delegate his faculty for granting this indulgence, even though it is an ordinary power of jurisdiction.[57] All in the abbot's separated territory can gain the indulgence, even the exempt religious.[58]

A doubt arose regarding canon 349, § 2, 2°, as to whether a bishop was forbidden to grant the indulgence of fifty[59] days to exempt religious, or in their churches. The Pontifical Commission for Interpretation replied that he was not forbidden to do so.[60] This ruling applies also to the abbot *nullius*. Consequently he can grant this indulgence to the exempt religious in his territory, or in their churches.

Secondly, the abbot *nullius* can grant a plenary indulgence through the papal blessing which he can give twice a year, on two of the more solemn days of the year.[61]

Through canon 916 the abbot *nullius* receives the power to designate a privileged altar in his abbatial church, and in the parish churches of his territory. He can designate only one altar in each church, which altar he designates for all time as a daily privileged altar.

Finally, when an abbot *nullius* in virtue of the authorization given him by canon 323, § 2, consecrates a church or an immovable altar, he can grant an indulgence of one year. This indulgence the faithful can gain only on the day of consecration by making a visit to the church or altar. On the anniversary of the dedication he can grant an indulgence of fifty days, under the same conditions.[62] Even through the granting

[57] Can. 913, 1° and 2°.

[58] Can. 927.

[59] Now of 100 days.—Sacra Poenitentiaria, decr. 20 iul. 1942—*AAS*, XXXIV (1942), 240; *The Jurist*, III (1943), 157.

[60] P.C.I., 6 dec. 1930—*AAS*, XXIII (1931), 25; *Periodica*, XX (1931), 148.

[61] Can. 914; Sacra Poenitentiaria, decr. 20 iul. 1942—*AAS*, XXXIV (1942), 240; *The Jurist*, III (1943), 157. Cf. also *supra*, p. 4.

[62] Can. 1166, § 3. The decree of the Sacred Penitentiary (20 July, 1942—*AAS*, XXXIV [1942], 240) which allows the abbot *nullius* to grant an

of the indulgence is considered as the fulfillment of a law, the indulgence cannot be understood to be automatically granted; it must be granted formally and proclaimed each time it is granted.[63]

Some doubt may arise as to whether the abbot *nullius* can grant the indulgences of canon 1166, § 3, in view of the restriction of canon 912, which demands that the power to grant indulgences must be expressly given by law. Canon 1166 does not expressly mention the abbot *nullius*.

To settle this doubt, no argument can be formed from the presumption established in canon 323, § 1, for this presumption fails in the light of canon 912. Other proofs must therefore be sought.

Upon inspection of the terms in canon 1166, § 3, it is found that the power to grant the indulgences is expressly granted to the *episcopus consecrator*. The abbot, however, is included under this term by the force of canon 215, § 2, and 323, § 2. Neither the wording of canon 1166, § 3, nor the nature of the consideration seem to exclude him. On the contrary, canon 323, § 2, rather tends to include him under this term.

Furthermore, a cardinal who is not a bishop can consecrate a church and grant indulgences only because the law expressly permits him to do so.[64] Yet canon 1166, § 3, in its last phrase, definitely shows that a cardinal is included under the term *episcopus consecrator*. Since the abbot *nullius*, like the cardinal, obtains his power to consecrate and to grant indulgences only from the law, he likewise should be included under the term *episcopus consecrator*.[65]

indulgence of 100 days instead of 50, cannot be extended in its application to canon 1166, § 3. For the decree itself is issued only in relation to canon 323, § 2, which is specifically mentioned in the decree. The indulgence of canon 1166, § 3, is different from that of canon 323, § 2, for it is granted only on the anniversary of a church dedication.

63 Vermeersch-Creusen, *Epitome,* II, 483.

64 Cans. 239, 20°; 912.

65 It appears that the term *episcopus consecrator* includes all those who can consecrate a church or an altar in virtue of their ordinary power of orders. Those who consecrate through delegated powers cannot grant this indulgence,

To these arguments may be added the fact that the granting of this indulgence is part of the ceremony of consecration.[66] Since the legislator gave the abbot *nullius* the power to consecrate a church, he would hardly intend to exclude the granting of the indulgences pertaining to the consecration.[67]

Consequently it is concluded that an abbot *nullius* can grant the indulgences mentioned in canon 1166, § 3. Most of the authors do not even mention this point. Those who do, however, maintain that the abbot *nullius* can grant these indulgences.[68]

These then are the powers for the granting of indulgences that an abbot *nullius* has by reason of his office.

but only proclaim it. — "... Indulgentiae in consecratione altaris conceduntur ab episcopo qui altare consecrat, vel consecrare deberet, et tantum promulgantur ab ipso delegato."—S.R.C., 26 oct. 1931 (private response)—*Archiv für katholisches Kirchenrecht*, CXIII (1933), 115; Bouscaren, *Canon Law Digest*, I, 560.

[66] Pontificale Romanum, tit. *De Dedicatione Ecclesiae.*

[67] "Cui licet, quod est plus, licet utique quod est minus." — Reg. 53, R.J., in VI°.

[68] Coronata, *Institutiones*, n. 737; Jone, *Gesetzbuch des kanonischen Rechtes*, II, 365.

CHAPTER V

HONORIFIC RIGHTS AND PRIVILEGES

Thus far this dissertation has treated the various powers that the law gives to the abbot *nullius*, and the obligations that it imposes upon him. The present chapter will deal with his honorific rights and privileges. Nothing will be said of any special rights or privileges that he may possess either through a specific grant of the Holy See, or through the privileges granted to his religious order. Here will be considered only those honorific rights and privileges which are attributed to him by the common law of the Code.

ARTICLE I. PRECEDENCE

Precedence, in law, connotes the honorific right by which an ecclesiastical dignitary occupies a specific place of honor or distinction among other ecclesiastical dignitaries.[1] It denotes, as it were, "a priority in rank or dignity."[2] This right of precedence determines just what place a dignitary will occupy at a council, in a public procession, or in any other official public gathering. The purpose of precedence looks to the achievement of having everything well ordered at all public assemblies, so that the most honored ecclesiastical dignitary will occupy the foremost place, the next in honor the second place, and so on, the same equitable proportion being observed for all alike down to the lowliest cleric. What the most honored place is depends on the particular function that is taking place. In church, for instance, the most honored place is the one which

[1] Augustine, *A Commentary on the New Code of Cannon Law*, II, 36; Beste, *Introductio in Codicem*, p. 162; Coronata, *Institutiones*, n. 155; Tamburini, *De Jure Abbatum*, tom. I, disput. XXV, quaes. I, n. 67. Cf. also c. 1, X, *de maioritate et obedientia*, I, 33.

[2] Augustine, *loc. cit.*

is nearest the altar and on the gospel side; in a procession with the Blessed Sacrament the most honored place is the one which is nearest the Blessed Sacrament, and so on. The place of honor is usually .determined by liturgical law.

A. PRECEDENCE OUTSIDE OF THE TERRITORY

The Code has specifically legislated on the precedence of some dignitaries, such as the Cardinals, Papal Legates, Patriarchs, etc.[3] But no such legislation has been made concerning the abbot *nullius.* Consequently, to determine his right of precedence, one must apply the general norms given in canon 106.

The first principle of precedence is that he who holds authority over persons, either physical or moral, also holds the right of precedence over these persons.[4] However, in assemblies outside of his separated territory the abbot *nullius* will be among persons over whom he holds no authority. Hence his right of precedence in such cases will be determined according to his rank (*gradus*). The principle which then obtains is this: those of a higher rank precede those of lower rank.[5] There is some controversy as to the meaning of the word "*gradus.*" Some authors hold that it refers to the degree of jurisdiction that is possessed.[6] If this were true, then in determining the right of precedence of an abbot *nullius,* one would have to take into consideration the kind of jurisdiction the abbot holds. The fact that he partakes of the papal jurisdiction would in some way influence the view on his right of precedence. The more tenable opinion is that "*gradus*" in canon 106 refers rather to the degree of preeminence consequent to some title or honor.[7] *Gradus* can hardly be referred to jurisdiction, for precedence by jurisdiction is taken care of in number 2 of canon 106. Nor can *gradus* be refered to orders, for precedence

[3] Cans. 239, § 1, 21°; 269, § 2; 280; 370, § 1.

[4] Can. 106, 2°.

[5] Can. 106, 3°.

[6] Coronata, *Institutiones,* n. 157; Woywod, *A Practical Commentary on the Code of Canon Law,* I, 47.

[7] Vermeersch-Creusen, *Epitome,* I, n. 230; Vermeersch, "Annotationes," (ad responsa varia Comm. Codicis Interpr.)—*Periodica,* XIV (1925), 180.

according to orders is treated later in number 3 of the same canon, where it is stated that dignitaries of the same rank but of a higher order precede those of a lower order. *Gradus*, therefore, is to be referred to rank, which is something altogether distinct from both jurisdiction and orders. Hence, Cardinals, Primates, Bishops, Monsignors, and so on, are of a different rank. Their jurisdictional powers, whatever these may be, do not enter into determining their right of precedence according to number 3 of canon 106.

The question to be here determined is this: just where in an assembly which represents various ranks does the rank of an abbot *nullius* belong. The old law offers no solution, for it completely lacks any general principles on precedence. Besides, in the Code the laws on precedence are such as to revise the entire matter of the former law.[8] Tradition, however, ranks the abbot immediately after the bishop. At the Council of Trent, for instance, where the question of precedence had to be settled, the abbots were placed immediately after the bishops.[9] From that time on the abbatial rank was always looked upon as immediately following upon the rank of a bishop.[10] Since the abbot *nullius* is of a higher rank than the

[8] Can. 22. "Codicem autem immutasse de facto ius antea in hac parte vigens, res est manifesta; immo leges de praecedentia in Codice contentae sunt et apparent ex illis legibus quae 'totam de integro ordinant legis prioris materiam' (can. 22), et ideo ad normam can. 6, n. 1, quaslibet leges sive particulares sive contrarias omnino abrogant. Enimvero in Codice primum (can. 106) inveniuntur normae generales, perspicuae illae ac omnino rationabiles, hanc materiam ordinantes, quae singulis locis variis muneribus applicantur, utpote nominatim in can. 370 .... Frustra quid simile perquires in toto corpore iuris ... ubi nonnisi lacinias invenies, praeter quas, ad moderandum ius praecedentiae, non supererat nisi congeries resolutionum S.R.C., atque usus et observantia."—S.C.C., *Cuneen. et Utinen.*, 17 maii, 1919—*AAS*, XI (1919), 352. The quotation is from the *animadversiones* of the Consultor.

[9] Barbosa, *Iuris Ecclesiastici Universi Libri Tres*, lib. I, c. XVII, nos. 1, 2, 3, 115; Fagnanus, *Commentaria in quinque Libros Decretalium*, in c. 1 (*Ut abbates*), X, *de aetate et qualitate, et ordine praeficiendorum*, I, 14, nn. 17–18.

[10] Molitor, *Religiosi Iuris Capita Selecta*, p. 402; Tamburini, *De Jure Abbatum*, tom. 1, disput. XXIV, quaes. III, n. 4; disput. XXV, quaes. II, n. 14; disput. XXV, quaes. III, n. 1.

ordinary abbot in his own right, the abbot *nullius* will precede other abbots, and hence follow immediately after the bishops. The Code itself illustrates the fact that the rank of an abbot *nullius* immediately follows upon the rank of a bishop. When the canons which deal with the matter of precedence[11] are compared with the canons wherein the various ranks are enumerated in order,[12] it becomes evident that the various ranks of ecclesiastical dignity are enumerated in the order of their precedence. In all these enumerations the abbot *nullius* is placed immediately after the bishop,[13] or immediately after those who represent the bishop or hold an episcopal office,[14] in accord with canon 106, n. 1.

From this it appears manifest that the rank of an abbot *nullius* follows immediately upon the rank of a bishop. Among several abbots *nullius*, precedence will be reckoned in relation to the point of time at which the one received his office earlier than the other, *i.e.*, reckoned to the very day when he received his office from the Sacred Consistorial Congregation.[15]

B. PRECEDENCE WITHIN THE TERRITORY

In his own separated territory the abbot *nullius* will precede all his subjects, because he holds jurisdiction over them.[16] However, a difficulty arises whenever other such abbots and bishops are assembled in the separated territory. Then there is the problem whether the abbot *nullius*, in his own separated territory, precedes all, even the visiting bishops. In other words, the point at issue is whether the rule of canon 347 is to be applied also to the abbot *nullius*.

[11] Cans. 239, § 1, 21°; 269, § 2; 280, et alii.

[12] E.g., cans. 120, § 2; 223; 282, § 1.

[13] E.g., cans. 120, § 1; 223, § 1.

[14] E.g., can. 282, § 1, where the coadjutor and apostolic administrator are listed before the abbot *nullius*.

[15] "Utrum vi canonis 106, 3°, praecedentia inter Episcopos suffraganeos in Concilio provinciali aliisque coetibus provincialibus definienda sit a die praeconizationis . . . an a die promotionis ad Ecclesiam suffraganeam. R: Affirmative ad primam partem, negative ad secundam.—P.C.I., 10 nov. 1925 —*AAS*, XVII (1925), 582.

[16] Can. 106, 2°.

According to canon 347 a diocesan bishop in his own diocese has the right of precedence over everyone, except Cardinals, Papal Legates, and his own Metropolitan. Is this right also to be extended to the abbot *nullius?* Authors do not give any consideration to this particular point; neither has the Holy See as yet issued a definite response in this matter. Nevertheless, it is here maintained that canon 347 does give the abbot *nullius* the right of precedence over everyone in his territory, except the three dignitaries specifically mentioned in canon 347.

The basis for this assertion is found in canon 215, § 2, where it is stated that in the Code the word "bishop" includes the abbot *nullius*, unless the nature of the matter at hand, or the context of the pertinent law exclude the abbot. This immediately establishes the presumption that in canon 347 the word "bishop" includes the abbot *nullius*, unless the contrary is proved. To prove the contrary, however, one would have to prove that either the context of the given law does not permit the inclusion of the abbot *nullius*, or that the nature of the situation demands his exclusion. It must also be remembered that according to the view of a consultor of the Sacred Congregation of the Council,[17] the Code laws on precedence deal with the entire matter of the former law in the sense explained by canon 22, and by such a re-ordering of the previous enactments in reality effects their total abrogation to favor the independent existence of the present Code law. Consequently, it is highly inadvisable to adduce arguments, for or against, from pre-Code legislation, except perhaps some responses from the Sacred Congregation of Rites.

The context of canon 347 certainly does not tend to exclude the abbot *nullius*. The nature of the situation, far from excluding the abbot *nullius*, rather includes him. The reason is that precedence in general attaches to the office.[18] The right

[17] S.C.C., *Cuneen. et Utinen.*, 17 maii 1919—*AAS*, XI (1919), 349–354. Cf. also note 8.

[18] "... e contrario praecedentia statuitur inter munera, officia, qualitates, in abstracto (v. gr. antianitas, ordo sacerdotalis, etc.)."—S.C.C., *Cuneen. et Utinen.*, 17 maii 1919—*AAS*, XI (1919), 351.

of precedence mentioned in canon 347 is therefore given to the bishop not because of his consecration, but because of his office. It is not something personal, but something that goes with the episcopal office, and is definitely attached to the episcopal office. But the office of abbot *nullius* is likewise an office which in law is recognized as equivalent to the episcopal office, since such an abbot has all the jurisdictional rights and obligations of a diocesan bishop, can have a vicar general, and so on.[19] Furthermore, it is a general rule, that by virtue of canon 215, § 2, the rights and privileges that accrue to a diocesan bishop by reason of his office, and not by reason of his consecration, accrue also to the abbot *nullius*.[20] If, then, the precedence in canon 347 is attached to the episcopal office, it must likewise be attached to the office of an abbot *nullius*. Since, therefore, neither the context in the text of canon 347, nor the nature of the situation demands otherwise, the word "bishop" in canon 347 includes the abbot *nullius*, and that by virtue of the presumption established by the force of canon 215, § 2.

Furthermore, since the abbot *nullius* assumes all the duties of a diocesan bishop, he should aslo enjoy the honorific rights of a diocesan bishop, as much as possible.[21]

From this it is concluded that within his own separated territory the abbot *nullius*, by force of canon 347, has the right to precede all, even visiting bishops and archbishops, except Cardinals, Papal Legates, and his own Metropolitan.[22]

[19] Can. 323, §§ 1 and 3.

[20] "Volumus autem ut Tu in tuae Abbatiae territorium et in personas ibi degentes eamden tum ordinis tum iurisdictionis exerceas potestatem, quam Episcopi in propriis dioecesibus et eorumdem iuribus fruaris ac legibus et officiis adstringaris, iis vero exceptis, ad quae exercenda character episcopalis requiritur."—Cancellaria Apostolica, 12 dec. 1924—Original document of the confirmation of the election of Abbot Vincent Taylor, O.S.B., of Belmont Abbey *Nullius*, Belmont, N.C.

[21] "Qui sentit onus, sentire debet commodum, et e contra."—Reg. 55, R.J., in VI°.

[22] Can. 347; cf. also can. 285, which orders such abbots to choose metropolitans.

One should note that canon 347 gives the abbot the right to precede all in his separated territory, but does not strictly demand the use of this right as a means for fulfilling an imposed obligation. In practice, and outside of formal functions, it is quite customary to honor visiting prelates by allowing them to have the more honored places.[23]

Article II. Privileges Regarding Trials

A. Privileges of the Forum

The privilege of the forum, as enjoyed by all clerics, exempts them from the jurisdiction of the secular courts. The principles of this privilege are enunciated in canon 120, where it is stated that no cleric can be summoned as a defendant before any secular tribunal. All clergy, even those who have only received the first tonsure,[24] enjoy this privilege. The abbot *nullius*, however, enjoys this privilege to a greater extent than the lower clergy, in so far as he is specifically enumerated among the higher dignitaries. These cannot be summoned as defendants to secular courts without the permission of the Holy See, whereas the lower clergy may be summoned with the permission of their bishop.

It is to be further noted that the canon says *conveniri nequeunt*. The word *convenire* in its technical sense means to summon to court as a defendant. This then is the only capacity in which a cleric cannot be summoned to a civil court. The canon by no means prohibits the abbot *nullius* to appear in a civil court as plaintiff or witness.[25] This conclusion can also be based on the principle that the plaintiff follows the tribunal of the defendant.[26] Consequently the permission of

[23] *Declarationes et Statuta Congregationis Americano-Cassinensis*, n. 83; Wernz-Vidal, *Ius Canonicum*, II, 636.

[24] Can. 108, § 1.

[25] Coronata, *Institutiones*, n. 183; Lega-Bartoccetti, *Commentarius in Iudicia Ecclesiastica* (3 vols., Romae: Anonima Libraria Cattolica Italiana, 1938–1941), I, 87.

[26] Can. 1559, § 3.

the Holy See is required only if someone wishes to lodge a charge against the abbot *nullius* in a secular court. If the abbot himself is the plaintiff, or if he is summoned as a witness, no such permission is required.

Failure to comply with the provisions of canon 120 exposes the guilty party to the penalties of canon 2341.

B. PRIVILEGES IN ECCLESIASTICAL COURTS

In the treatise on the competent tribunal the Code reserves some cases personally to the Holy Father, while it reserves others to the tribunals of the Holy See.[27] Any other ecclesiastical tribunal is absolutely incompetent in these cases.

Among the cases reserved personally to the Holy Father are the criminal trials of bishops.[28] The question is whether the word "bishop" in this canon includes the abbot *nullius*, thereby also reserving criminal trials involving him as a defendant to the Roman Pontiff.

At first sight it would seem that such abbots are here included under the term "bishop," precisely in view of the rule expressed in canon 215, § 2. However, upon closer consideration they must be excluded. The whole first paragraph of canon 1557 enumerates definite persons whose trials are reserved to the Holy Father, and the reservations are based on the dignity of the persons.[29] Regarding the bishops, the reservation is accordingly established in view of the episcopal character,[30] which is obtained through episcopal consecration. Consequently under the term "bishop" there can come only those who have episcopal consecration, regardless of whether they do or do not have any jurisdictional rights. The fact that titular bishops are included further corroborates this view. Even Archbishops, Patriarchs, and Primates come under this canon only by reason

[27] Can. 1557.

[28] Can. 1557, § 1, 3°.

[29] Lega-Bartoccetti, *Commentarius in Iudicia Ecclesiastica*, I, 33.

[30] Roberti, *De Processibus* (ed. altera, Romae: apud Aedes Facultatis Iuridicae ad S. Apollinaris, 1941–?), p. 185.

of their episcopal character and dignity of person. Hence the abbot *nullius*, since he lacks episcopal consecration, must be excluded. If however he has received episcopal consecration, he enjoys the concession of canon 1557, § 1, 3°.

Furthermore, this canon enumerates classes of persons who are exempted from subjection to the general competency of ecclesiastical tribunals in view of their personal dignity.[31] Now, according to canon 19, any law which proposes an exception to the generally obtaining rule must be interpreted strictly, and for that reason the listing of the excepted persons must be regarded as all-inclusive, and not merely as demonstrative in character. It therefore appears conclusive that the term "bishop" does not comprise in its concept the abbot *nullius*. Hence in criminal trials the latter's case is not reserved personally to the Holy Father. Roberti teaches that in criminal cases such abbots and prelates are subject to the *tribunals* of the Holy See.[32]

The second paragraph of canon 1557 deals with the cases reserved to the tribunals of the Holy See. Here it is stated that in contentious trials the passing of judgment on residential bishops is reserved to the tribunals of the Apostolic See. The same question again arises, namely, whether the word "bishop" here includes the abbot *nullius*. The answer is that the abbot is here included under the term "bishop" in virtue of canon 215, § 2. Canon 1557, § 2, 1°, speaks of residential bishops, thereby showing that it is not by reason of the episcopal character, but rather by reason of the episcopal office that contentious trials involving a bishop as defendant are reserved to the Roman tribunals. Hence titular bishops are excluded from the scope of this reservation.[33] Furthermore, the canon also allows contentious cases of the residential bishop, if they deal with his temporal goods, to be judged by the diocesan tribunal, but

[31] Lega-Bartoccetti, *Commentarius in Iudicia Ecclesiastica*, I, 33.

[32] Roberti, *De Processibus*, I (ed. 1941?), 185. The 1926 edition does not mention this point.

[33] Lega-Bartoccetti, *Commentarius in Iudicia Ecclesiastica*, I, 36; Vermeersch-Creusen, *Epitome*, III, n. 14.

with the consent of the bishop.[34] Among authors it is the common opinion that the term "bishop" in canon 1557, § 2, 1°, includes the abbot *nullius*.[35]

Hence according to canons 215, § 2, and 1557, § 2, 1°, the contentious cases of the abbot *nullius* are reserved to the tribunals of the Holy See. Neither the context of canon 1557, § 2, 1°, nor the nature of the situation tend to exclude the abbot from the term "bishop." Rather, as was shown above, they tend to include him.

To summarize, the abbot's privileges, as far as court procedures are concerned, are only two. First, he cannot be summoned as a defendant to the secular tribunal without the permission of the Holy See. Secondly, in contentious trials as well as in criminal trials[36] the passing of judgment on him is reserved to the tribunals of the Holy See.

Article III. Privileges Regarding Burial

The abbot *nullius* enjoys two privileges regarding burial. First, he has the right to choose his burial place, and secondly he may be buried within the abbatial church.

All the faithful, unless they are expressly prohibited from so doing by law, have the right to choose the church from which, and the cemetery in which they wish to be buried.[37] But professed religious no longer enjoy this right,[38] and must be buried from the churches of their own religious order.[39]

The abbot *nullius*, however, can choose the place of his burial. Even though he is usually a professed religious, he still falls under the general rule of canon 1224, § 2, which per-

[34] Cans. 1557, § 2, 1°; 1572, § 2.

[35] Coronata, *Institutiones*, n. 1097, note 8; Roberti, *De Processibus*, I (ed. 1941?), 185.

[36] Roberti, *De Processibus*, I (ed. 1941?), 185.

[37] Can. 1223, § 1.

[38] Can. 1224, § 2.

[39] Can. 1221, § 1.

mits religious bishops to choose the place of their burial. For under the term "bishop" must also be included the abbot *nullius*, since there is no reason according to the norms of canon 215, § 2, for excluding him. In fact, canon 1219 further corroborates this view by definitely allowing the abbot *nullius* to choose the church from which he wishes to be buried.[40]

This therefore is the first privilege regarding burial, namely, that the abbot *nullius* can choose the church and cemetery for his burial. If he does not make this choice, then he is to be buried from his abbatial church,[41] and according to the constitutions, if any such exist, of his order.

The second privilege regarding burial is that the abbot *nullius* may be buried within the abbatial church.[42] The Church has from early times prohibited the burial of the dead within the edifice of a consecrated church.[43] Canon 1205, § 2, still forbids this practice, and only by way of exception does it allow certain ecclesiastical dignitaries to be buried in a church. The abbot *nullius* is specifically enumerated among these dignitaries. The canon rules that these may be buried in a church, but only in their own churches. Hence, if the abbot *nullius* is to be buried within a church, it must be his own abbatial church, and not any other church.

No specific place where the corpse may be laid in the church is indicated in any positive manner. There is a negative indication, however, in as far as no corpse may be buried di-

40 Can. 1219, § 2; Coronata, *Institutiones*, n. 801 *b*); Vermeersch-Creusen, *Epitome*, II, n. 530.

41 Can. 1219, § 2; Vermeersch-Creusen (*Epitome*, II, n. 530) hold that the abbatial church, as well as the cathedral church for the bishop, are given preference over the *sepulchrum maiorum*, as churches from which the funeral is to be conducted. The order, then, would be as follows: the church chosen; the abbatial church; the *sepulchrum maiorum*.

42 Can. 1205, § 2.

43 C. 15, 18, C. XIII, q. 2; "... ideo prohibetur fieri sepultura in ecclesia, quia locus ille specialiter Deo dedicatus est: cui mors ultra non dominabitur."—*Glossa ordinaria* in v. *sepeliantur*, c. 15, C. XIII, q. 2.

rectly under the altar.[44] It may be buried near the altar, one foot away from the *mensa* of the altar, or, if it be a portable altar, one foot away from the table upon which the portable altar is resting.[45]

These, then, are the abbot's privileges regarding burial. He may first choose the church from which, and the cemetery in which, he is to be buried, and secondly he may, if he so desires, be buried within his abbey church.

Article IV. Pontifical Rights and Privileges

Canon 325: Abbas vel Praelatus *nullius*, licet charactere episcopali careat, utitur tamen in proprio territorio insignibus pontificalibus cum throno ac baldachino et iure ibidem officia divina pontificali ritu celebrandi; crucem autem pectoralem, annulum cum gemma, ac pileolum violaceum potest etiam extra territorium deferre.

The abbot *nullius* is equivalent to a diocesan bishop, as far as jurisdiction and obligations are concerned.[46] Canon 325 further concedes to such abbots some of the pontifical rights which normally are proper to the bishop only. It allows the abbot *nullius* to use certain pontifical insignia, and to perform some liturgical functions according to the pontifical rite. Specifically, canon 325 allows the following:

1) The abbot *nullius* may use the pontifical insignia, *i.e.*, the miter and the crosier.[47] These he may use only in his own separated territory.

2) He may use the episcopal throne and baldachin, but again only in his own territory.

3) The abbot has the right to perform liturgical functions according to the pontifical rite, but likewise only in his territory.

[44] Can. 1202, § 2.
[45] Can. 1202, § 2; Coronata, *Institutiones*, n. 773.
[46] Can. 323, § 1.
[47] Can. 337, § 2.

4) Finally, he may wear the pectoral cross, the pontifical ring, and a purple skull cap. These he may wear even outside of his separated territory.

It is to be noted that the abbot's pontifical rights differ to some extent from those of a bishop. The main difference is that a bishop may pontificate in another diocese, provided he has the consent of that ordinary.[48] The abbot *nullius* on the other hand is not able to pontificate outside of his territory, for canon 325 seems to restrict the abbot's pontifical functions only to his own separated territory.[49] This territorial restriction gives rise to the question whether the abbot *nullius* can pontificate in another exempt monastery that is situated within the confines of his territory. The question is not directly answered in canon 325. The bishop, however, according to canon 337, § 1, can pontificate in his whole diocese, including the exempt monasteries. The abbot *nullius*, according to canon 325, may also pontificate in his whole territory, but no mention is made of the exempt places in his territory. Nevertheless, such exempt places are still a part of his territory, and while pontificating there, he would still pontificate in his own territory. Hence, as the bishop in the light of the canon 337, § 1, can pontificate in exempt monasteries of his diocese, so the abbot *nullius* may also pontificate in the exempt monasteries of his separated territory.[50] The formal con-

[48] Can. 337, § 1.

[49] "Abbas vel Praelatus *nullius*, ... utitur ... iure *ibidem* (italics inserted) officia divina pontificali ritu celebrandi; ..."—can. 325. Cf. also S.R.C., *Barchinonen.*, 11 iul. 1739—*Decreta Authentica Congregationis Sacrorum Rituum ex actis eiusdem collecta cura et studio Aloisii Gardellini* (3. ed., 4 vols., Romae, 1856–1858), n. 4089, henceforth referred to as *Decr. Auth.* S.R.C.; S.R.C., *Bahien. in Brasilia*, 23 maii 1846—*Decr. Auth.* S.R.C., n. 5038; S.R.C., *Tortonen.*, 12 sept. 1671—*Decr. Auth.* S.R.C., n. 2562; (Anonymous), "Use of Pontificals by Benedictine Abbots,"—*ER*, CVIII (1943), 454–456. Some authors, however, appeal to custom, and claim that any abbot, if invited by a bishop into his diocese, may perform pontifical functions there. Cf. Augustine, *Rights and Duties of Ordinaries* (St. Louis, Mo.: B. Herder Book Co., 1924), p. 39.

[50] Compare cans. 20; 325; 337, § 1.

sent of the religious superior of the exempt monastery is not required. The superior's consent is required only when an extra-diocesan bishop wishes to pontificate in the monastery.[51] The abbot *nullius* may, therefore, pontificate in an exempt monastery, provided that it is located within his territory. He does not need the superior's formal permission.

It is further to be observed that the abbot *nullius* receives these pontifical rights and privileges directly from his office. Even though he lacks episcopal consecration, he nevertheless still enjoys the rights enumerated in canon 325. All that is required is that he receive the office canonically, and is duly installed into office.[52] Hence he may exercise these rights even before he has received the abbatial blessing, and immediately after his installation in office, if this should happen to take place before the abbatial blessing is received. On the contrary, the governing abbot in a religious order indeed enjoys these same privileges,[53] but only after he has received the abbatial blessing.[54] In this latter case the privileges result from the abbatial blessing, and are, as it were, attached to the abbatial blessing. But in the case of an abbot *nullius* they are attached to the office, and in no way depend on the abbatial blessing.

Two other liturgical privileges are granted by the Code to the abbot *nullius*. He may wear his purple skull cap and ring while celebrating mass,[55] and he is allowed to have an assisting priest at his mass.[56]

[51] Can. 337, § 1.

[52] Can. 322, § 1; cf. *supra*, page 45.

[53] Can. 625. The abbot of a monastery cannot wear the purple skull cap (can. 625); but he may wear a black one—S.R.C., 31 iul. 1929—*Periodica*, XVIII (1929), 245.

[54] Can. 625.

[55] Can. 811, § 2.

[56] Can. 812. For specific liturgical rules on the pontifical functions permitted to these abbots, cf. Martinucci, *Manuale Sacrarum Caeremoniarum* (3. ed., II partes in 4 vols., Romae: Pustet, 1911–1915), Pars II, Vol. II, 692 ff. (appendix to lib. VIII). Cf. also Ahearne-Lane, *Pontifical Ceremonies* (London and Dublin: Burns, Oates & Washbourne, Ltd., 1942).

It seems advisable to mention at least that canon 349 extends quite a few privileges to the bishop. These, however, can in no way be extended to the abbot *nullius*. The privileges mentioned in canon 349, § 1, 1°, are granted personally to bishops, either residential or titular. The rest of the rights and privileges enumerated therein are, as far as the abbot *nullius* is concerned, properly adverted to in other canons.[5] Consequently there can be no doubt that canon 349 does not apply to the abbot *nullius*, but only to a bishop in view of his consecration.

57 Cans. 323, § 2; 294, § 2; 325.

CHAPTER VI

ADMINISTRATION OF THE SEPARATED TERRITORY

The abbot *nullius* has both the right and the duty to govern the separated territory in matters spiritual as well as temporal, through his judicial, legislative, and coercive powers.[1] The separated territory will, therefore, be administered in the same manner as a diocese. Hence the abbot appoints a court with all its officials, and establishes a diocesan curia with all the personnel pertinent thereto, or, if the territory is rather small, he appoints as many officials to his curia as are necessary to carry on the normal business of his chancery.

ARTICLE I. THE VICAR GENERAL

Canon 323, § 3: Quod attinet ad Vicarii Generalis constitutionem, serventur praescripta can. 366–371.

According to this canon, should the size of the separated territory and the multiple burdens resulting from the office demand it, the abbot may freely appoint a vicar general.[2] If circumstances demand it, he may even appoint more than one vicar general.[3]

The vicar general of a separated territory, by reason of his office, holds the same jurisdiction as the abbot *nullius*. The only difference is that the abbot exercises a *proper* ordinary power, while the vicar general exercises a *vicarious* ordinary power. For two reasons the vicar general's ordinary power may be curtailed: first, if the abbot deems it advisable to restrict the use of certain jurisdictional powers to himself, and

[1] Cans. 323, § 1; 335, § 1.

[2] Cans. 323, § 3; 366, §§ 1 and 2.

[3] Can. 366, § 3.

secondly, if the law itself demands a special mandate for the vicar general.[4] The cases wherein the law demands this special mandate are explicitly indicated in the Code under the various canons.[5]

Canon 323, § 3, further indicates that the vicar general of a separated territory is equivalent to the vicar general of a diocese. Hence the vicar general of a separated territory must possess the same qualifications, but he enjoys the same rights and is held to the same duties as the diocesan vicar general. In only one respect do the two differ. The diocesan vicar general is to be selected from the secular clergy,[6] while the vicar general of a separated territory may be a religious, and of the same religious order as is the abbot who is in charge of the separated territory.[7] In everything else the vicar general of a separated territory, like the diocesan vicar general, is ruled by canons 366–371.[8]

Article II. The Chapter

The abbot *nullius* is a major religious superior and at the same time a local ordinary. When he assumes the office of an abbot *nullius*, in addition to his rights and duties as a major religious superior, he likewise assumes the rights and duties of the office of an abbot *nullius*. Both offices are vested in the same person. Similarly, the religious chapter, which assists the abbot in ruling the monastic family, automatically assumes the responsibilities of a diocesan chapter whenever the abbot

[4] Can. 368, § 1.

[5] E.g., cans. 113; 357, § 2; 455, § 3, etc. A controversy exists as to whether the vicar general acts by ordinary or delegated powers when he acts in virtue of this special mandate. Cf. Roelker, "The Vicar General and the Special Mandate"—*Jurist*, II (1942), 346–362.

[6] Can. 367, § 1.

[7] Can. 367, § 2.

[8] For a further study of the vicar general, cf. Campagna, *Il Vicario Generale del Vescovo* (The Catholic University of America Canon Law Studies, n. 66, Washington, D.C.: The Catholic University of America, 1931).

of its monastery becomes an abbot *nullius*. The religious chapter then acts both as a religious chapter, and as the equivalent of a cathedral chapter. The abbot need not have two distinct and separate chapters, one a religious and the other acting as a cathedral chapter. Rather, the religious chapter automatically assumes the duties which a cathedral chapter normally has.[9]

The superadded duties consist, in general, in assisting the abbot *nullius* in governing the separated territory, and in actually governing the territory upon the death of the abbot, until the chapter has elected an administrator for this purpose.[10] In some instances the Code demands that the abbot seek the advice of his chapter before he acts.[11] In other cases it requires that the abbot obtain the consent of his chapter in order to place his acts validly.[12] In this way the religious chapter will assist the abbot in governing the separated territory.

Regarding the laws by which this religious chapter is governed, canon 324 prescribes that it is governed by its own laws and religious constitutions. However, note must here be taken of canon 489, according to which particular constitutions conflicting with the Code are abrogated, unless the constitutions have been approved by Rome after 1918. Hence in all its dealings the religious chapter will first look to its constitutions, and then to the common law of the Code.

Nothing need be said of diocesan consultors. An abbot *nullius* will always have his religious chapter. The Code necessarily presupposes this, for it mentions consultors only in connection with a secular prelacy.[13]

[9] Cans. 324; 327, § 1; 391, § 1.

[10] Cans. 327, § 1; 391, § 1.

[11] E.g., cans. 403; 895. Cf. also can. 105. The cases and corresponding canons for which the advice or consent of the chapter is required are listed in Trombetta, *De Consensu et Consilio Capituli Cathedralis iuxta Codicem Iuris Canonici* (Neapoli: M. D'Auria, 1926), pp. 17–19, and 20–22.

[12] E.g., cans. 1532, § 3; 1541, § 2, 1. Cf. also Trombetta, *loc. cit.*

[13] Can. 326.

Parish consultors, the chancellor, and other officials of the curia in a separated territory have the same duties as these officials have in a diocese. They will be appointed in the same way, and governed by the same canons as the officials of a diocesan chancery.

Article III. Administration of the Territory when Vacant

Canon 327, § 1: Abbatia vel praelatura *nullius* vacante, si agatur de abbatia vel praelatura religiosa, succedit Capitulum religiosorum, nisi constitutionis aliud ferant; si de saeculari, Capitulum canonicorum; utrumque autem Capitulum intra octiduum debet Vicarium Capitularem deputare ad normam can. 432 seqq., qui abbatiam vel praelaturam regat usque ad novi Abbatis vel Praelati electionem.

Canon 327, § 1, offers two possibilities according to which the separated territory is administered when vacant. The first possibility allows the constitutions of the particular religious order to determine how the territory is to be governed. In the event that the constitutions are silent on this point, the administration of the vacant territory automatically devolves upon the religious chapter. The constitutions are preferred to the common law, and must be looked to first.

The constitutions which contain any ruling on this point normally designate a particular person, usually a superior, to whom the jurisdiction passes upon the death of the abbot. This is the case in the American-Cassinese Congregation of Benedictines. Their constitutions rule that upon the death of the abbot the jurisdiction devolves upon the prior of the monastery.[14] This same ruling of the constitutions will also

[14] "Ad eum (priorem) mortui Abbatis jurisdictio, donec in possessionem novus venerit, modo transit ordinario; . . ."—*Declarationes et Statuta Congregationis Americano-Cassinensis*, n. 90.

have force if the abbot is in charge of a separated territory.[15] Thus, when the abbot of Belmont Abbey dies,[16] his jurisdiction automatically devolves upon the prior. But if for some reason the prior could not take the office, the jurisdiction passes to the religious chapter, which will then elect an administrator,[17] in accord with the religious constitutions and canon 327, § 1.

The person to whom the constitutions entrust the jurisdiction receives it immediately upon the death of the abbot. Just what his powers are is not explicitly declared in the Code. He certainly does not have all the powers of the abbot *nullius*. But in the light of canon 20, that is, in dependence upon laws which are enacted for similar cases, it is quite certain that he will be equivalent to a diocesan administrator.[18] Hence his rights and duties will be determined from canons 429 - 444. He receives the ordinary jurisdiction of the abbot *nullius*, but not in its fullest extent, for in certain instances his jurisdictional powers are curtailed.[19] He will exercise this jurisdiction until the installation of the new abbot.[20]

A doubt may arise as to whether the religious chapter[21] must elect a vicar capitular even when the jurisdiction passes on to an individual, and not to the chapter. The election in this case is quite beyond the intention of canon 327, § 1. Like the secular chapter, the religious chapter elects an administrator only when the jurisdiction devolves upon the chapter it-

[15] Beste, *Introductio in Codicem*, p. 259; Jaeger, *The Administration of Vacant and Quasi-vacant Episcopal Sees in the United States* (The Catholic University of America Canon Law Studies, n. 81, Washington, D.C.: The Catholic University of America, 1932), p. 89.

[16] Belmont Abbey, Belmont, N.C., is the only abbey *nullius* in the United States.

[17] "... sed eo [priore] quacumque ex causa deficiente Administrator a conventu eligatur." — *Declarationes et Statuta Congregationis Americano-Cassinensis*, n. 90.

[18] Cans. 20; 327, § 1; 432, § 1; 435, § 1.

[19] Cf. cans. 113; 455, § 2; 893, § 1; 958, § 1, 3°, etc.

[20] Can. 443, § 2.

[21] "Utrumque autem Capitulum intra octiduum debet Vicarium Capitularem deputare ad normam can. 432 seqq. ..."—Can. 327, § 1.

self.[22] Whenever the jurisdiction is vested in an individual, he acts as administrator until the installation of the new abbot.

In the second possibility, whenever the constitutions do not make provision for the administrator of a vacant separated territory, the jurisdiction devolves upon the religious chapter. Immediately upon the death of the abbot the ordinary jurisdiction passes to the chapter, and for eight days the chapter may exercise this jurisdiction in the same manner, and with the same restrictions as an administrator.[23] Its most pressing duty, however, is to elect an administrator within eight days after the death of the abbot. Should the religious chapter fail in this respect, and should eight days elapse without any election of an administrator, the metropolitan of the separated territory will freely designate an administrator.[24] Once the administrator has been elected, or appointed by the metropolitan, the jurisdiction passes from the religious chapter to the newly elected administrator. The chapter can place no restrictions on the administrator's jurisdiction.[25] He needs no confirmation for his election, but immediately after his profession of faith, made before the chapter, he assumes the administration of the vacant territory.[26] From that point on the chapter simply assists the administrator in certain cases which demand the advice or consent of the chapter.[27] The chapter's next duty is to elect a new abbot.

The length of time during which the administrator holds his office is indicated in canon 327, § 1. This canon rules that the administrator holds office until the abbot's election.[28]

[22] Cans. 431, § 1; 432, § 2; Coronata, *Institutiones*, n. 461, *b*); Jaeger, *The Administration of Vacant and Quasi-vacant Episcopal Sees in the United States*, p. 89–90; Jone, *Gesetzbuch des kanonischen Rechtes*, I, 275; Wernz-Vidal, *Ius Canonicum*, II, 603.

[23] Can. 435.

[24] Can. 432, § 3. Cf. also can. 285.

[25] Can. 437.

[26] Can. 438; 1406, § 1, 4°.

[27] E.g., can. 113.

[28] "... qui abbatiam ... regat usque ad novi abbatis ... electionem."—Can. 327, § 1.

Taken in a strict canonical sense, this would mean that the administrator's office ceases when the newly elected abbot accepts the election. Who then would rule the separated territory until the abbot's installation? The abbot cannot exercise his jurisdiction before his corporeal installation in office.[29]

The word *electio* seems to have been poorly chosen in this canon. It must here be interpreted in a broader sense, and not in its strict canonical meaning.[30] Otherwise it not only leaves the separated territory without a head for a long time, but it also contradicts canon 443, § 2, which rules that the vicar capitular holds office until the installation of the bishop. Canon 443, § 2, applies also to the administrator of a separated territory, as is evident from canon 327, § 1. Hence, the word *electio* in canon 327, § 1, must be taken to mean the corporeal installation in office. The vicar capitular of a separated territory, then, administers the territory until the newly elected abbot is duly installed in office according to canon 322, § 1.

If at any time the administration of the separated territory should in some way be impeded, the norms of canon 429 are to be followed.[31]

These norms apply in such a contingency for the reason that a separated territory is equivalent to a diocese.[32] Fundamentally, then, the separated territory will be administered exactly as a diocese.

[29] Can. 322, § 1.

[30] Coronata, *Institutiones*, n. 390, note 10.

[31] Can. 327, § 2.

[32] Can. 215, § 2.

CONCLUSIONS

1) The essential factors in the creation of an abbacy or prelacy *nullius* are its actual separation from, and complete independence of, any diocese (can. 319).

2) The word "*nequit*" in canon 322, § 1, has an invalidating force. The abbot *nullius* cannot act validly before his corporeal installation in office, according to canon 322, § 1, and 334, § 3.

3) The omission of the profession of faith required by canon 1406, § 1, 3°, does not invalidate the tenure of the office.

4) The abbot *nullius* must also take the oath of fidelity to the Holy See. But the omission of this does not invalidate his incumbency in office.

5) Although canon 322, § 2, requires the abbatial blessing only of those who are commanded to receive it by a prescript of the Holy See, or by their constitutions, the canon must nevertheless be interpreted as including also those who are required by common law (can. 625) to receive the abbatial blessing.

6) By common law the special mandate of the Holy See for the blessing of an abbot is still required, even for an abbot *nullius*. The Benedictines, however, through a special privilege granted by Pope Benedict XV have this mandate *semel pro semper*.

7) Canon 323, § 2, is to be interpreted as meaning that all abbots and prelates *nullius* have the powers of both canon 294, § 2, and 323, § 2. Those, however, who must receive the abbatial blessing cannot use the powers of canon 323, § 2, *i.e.*, they cannot consecrate a church or an immovable altar until they have received the abbatial blessing.

8) The abbot *nullius*, when he consecrates a church or an immovable altar, can grant the indulgences of which canon 1166, § 3, makes mention.

9) Regarding precedence outside of his territory, the place of the abbot *nullius* is immediately after the bishops; in his own separated territory he has the right to precede all except Cardinals, Papal Legates, and his own Metropolitan (can. 347).

10) The trial of an abbot *nullius* in criminal matters is not reserved personally to the Roman Pontiff (can. 1557, § 1, n. 3). The trial of the abbot *nullius* in contentious matters is reserved to the tribunals of the Holy See.

11) The phrase *"usque ad novi Abbatis . . . electionem"* in canon 327, § 1, is to be understood as meaning "to the time of the corporeal installation of the new abbot," and not merely "to the time of his election." (can. 443, § 2).

BIBLIOGRAPHY

Sources

Acta Apostolicae Sedis, Commentarium Officiale, Romae, 1909–.

Acta et Decreta Concilii Plenarii Baltimorensis III, Baltimorae: Typis Joannis Murphy, 1886.

Acta Sanctae Sedis, 41 vols., Romae, 1865–1908.

Auvráy, Lucien, *Les Registres de Grégoire IX*, ed. Albert Fontemoing, 2 vols., Paris, 1896.

Bullarium Benedicti XIV (olim Prosperi Cardinalis de Lambertinis), 3 vols. (Vol. III in two parts), Prati: in Typographia Aldina, 1845–1847.

Bullarum Diplomatum et Privilegiorum Sanctorum Romanorum Pontificum Taurinensis Editio, 24 vols. et Appendix, Augustae Taurinorum—Neapoli, 1857–1872.

Bullarii Romani Continuatio, 19 vols. in 10, Romae, 1835–1857.

Codicis Iuris Canonici Fontes cura Emi. Petri Card. Gasparri editi, 9 vols., Romae (postea Civitate Vaticana): Typis Polyglottis Vaticanis, 1923–1939. (Vols. VII–IX, ed. cura et studio Emi. Justiniani Card. Seredi).

Corpus Iuris Canonici, 2. ed., Lipsiensis, post Aemilii Ludovici Richteri curas instruxit Aemilius Friedberg, 2 vols., Lipsiae, 1879–1881.

Declarationes et Statuta Congregationis Americano-Cassinensis, Atchison, Kansas: The Abbey Student Press, 1925.

Declarations and Constitutions of the Swiss-American Congregation, O.S.B., Conception, Mo.: Conception Abbey, 1938.

Decreta Authentica Congregationis Sacrorum Rituum ex actis eiusdem collecta cura et studio Aloisii Gardellini, 3. ed., 4 vols., Romae, 1856–1858.

Decretales D. Gregorii Papae IX, una cum Glossis Restitutae, Romae, 1582.

Decretum Gratiani emendatum et notationibus illustratum una cum Glossis, 2 vols., Romae, 1582.

Jaffé, Philippus, *Regesta Pontificum Romanorum ab condita ecclesia ad annum post Christum natum MCXCVIII*, 2. ed. correcta et aucta, 2 vols. in 1, Lipsiae, 1885–1888. (Ab condita ecclesia ad annum DXC, ed. F. Kaltenbrunner; ab anno DXC ad annum DCCCLXXXII, ed. P. Ewald; ab anno DCCCLXXXII ad annum MCXCVIII, ed. S. Loewenfeld.)

Kehr, Paulus F., *Italia Pontificia*, Tom. VIII. Regnum Normannorum-Campania (Regesta Pontificum Romanorum), Berolini: apud Weidmannos, 1935.

Liber Sextus Decretalium, una cum Clementinis et Extravagantibus earumque Glossis Restitutis, Romae, 1582.

Mansi, Ioannes, *Sacrorum Conciliorum Nova et Amplissima Collectio*, 53 vols. in 60, Parisiis, 1901–1927.

Monumenta Germaniae Historica, Gregorii I Papae Registrum Epistolarum, tom. I, ed. Paulus Ewald, Berolini: apud Weidmannos, 1887; tom. II, post P. Ewaldi obitum edidit Ludovicus Hartmann, Berolini: apud Weidmannos, pars I, 1893, pars 2, 1899.

————, *Scriptores*, tom. VII (folio), ed. Georgius Heinricus Pertz, Hannoverae, 1846; Unveränderter Neudruck, 1925.

Potthast, Augustus, *Regesta Pontificum Romanorum inde ab a. post Christum* natum *MCXCVIII ad a. MCCCIV*, 2 vols., Berolini, 1874–1875.

Sacrae Romanae Rotae Decisiones, coram P. Domino Cyriaco Lancetta, 7 vols., Romae, 1731–1735.

Sacrae Rotae Romanae Decisiones Nuperrimae, 9 vols. in 10, Romae, 1751–1763.

Sacrae Romanae Rotae Decisionum Recentiarum Partes, pars I, Francofurti, 1623; pars II, Aurelianae, 1623; partes III–XIX, Romae, 1645–1703.

Thesaurus Resolutionem Sacrae Congregationis Concilii, 167 vols., Romae, 1718–1908.

Reference Works

Ahearne, Pierce–Lane, Michael, *Pontifical Ceremonies*, London & Dublin: Burns, Oates & Washbourne, Ltd., 1942.

Augustine, Charles, *A Commentary on the New Code of Canon Law*, 8 vols., St. Louis, Mo.: Herder and Co., 1925–1938. Vol. I, 6. ed., 1931; Vol. II, 6. ed., 1936; Vol. III, 5. ed., 1938; Vol. IV, 3. ed., 1925; Vol. V, 5. ed., 1935; Vol. VI, 3. ed., 1931; Vol. VII, 3. ed., 1930; Vol. VIII, 3. ed., 1931.

————, *Rights and Duties of Ordinaries*, St. Louis, Mo.: Herder and Co., 1924.

Barbosa, Augustinus, *De Officio et Potestate Episcopi*, 2 vols., Lugduni, 1656.

————, *Iuris Ecclesiastici Universi Libri Tres*, ed. novissima, 2 vols., Lugduni, 1650–1660.

Baronius, Caesar, *Annales Ecclesiastici*, denuo excusi et ad nostra usque tempora perducti ab Augustino Theiner, 37 vols., Vols. I–XXVIII, Barri-Ducis, 1864–1875; Vols. XXIX–XXXVII, Parisiis, 1876–1883.

Bellarminus, Robertus, *Opera Omnia*, ed. nova, Parisiis, 1872.

Benedictus XIV, *De Synodo Dioecesana*, 2 vols., Parmae, 1764.

Beste, Udalricus, *Introductio in Codicem*, Collegeville, Minn.: St. John's Abbey Press, 1938.

Bouix, D., *De Jure Regularium,* 2 vols., Parisiis, 1857.

————, *Tractatus De Episcopo,* 2 vols., Parisiis, 1859.

Cappello, Felix, *Summa Iuris Canonici,* 3 vols., Romae: apud Aedes Universitatis Gregorianae, 1936–1939. Vol. I, 3. ed., 1938; Vol. II, 3. ed., 1939; Vol. III, 1936.

————, *Tractatus Canonico-Moralis de Sacramentis,* 3 vols. in 6, Romae: Marietti, 1932–1939. Vol. I, 3. ed., 1938; Vol. II, pars I, 3. ed., 1938; Vol. II, pars II, 1932; Vol. II, pars III, 1935; Vol. III, partes I–II, 4. ed., 1939.

Chelodi, Ioannes, *Ius De Personis,* ed. altera, Tridenti: Libr. Edit. Tridentum, 1927.

————, *Ius Poenale et Ordo Procedendi in Iudiciis Criminalibus iuxta Codicem Iuris Canonici,* Tridenti: Libr. Edit. Tridentum, 1925 (1920?).

Chokier, Erasmus, *De Jurisdictione Ordinarii in Exemptos,* Coloniae Agrippinae, 1629.

Coleman, John, *The Minister of Confirmation,* The Catholic University of America Canon Law Studies, n. 125, Washington, D.C.: The Catholic University of America Press, 1941.

Coronata, Matthaeus Conte a, *Institutiones Iuris Canonici,* 5 vols., Taurini, Romae: Marietti, 1933–1939. Vols. I, II, 2. ed., 1939; Vol. III, 1933; Vol. IV, 1935; Vol. V, 1936.

Creusen, Joseph–Garesche, Edward–Ellis, Adam, *Religious Men and Women in the Code,* 3. English ed., Milwaukee: The Bruce Publishing Co., 1940.

De Luca, Ioannes, *Theatrum Veritatis et Justitiae,* 16 vols. in 8, Coloniae Agrippinae, 1706.

De Prosperis, Josephus, *Tractatus de Territorio Separato,* Romae, 1712.

Devoti, Ioannes, *Institutionum Canonicarum Libri IV,* 2 vols., Leodii, 1860.

Dictionnaire de Droit Canonique, Paris, 1924–1937.

Duchesne, L., *Le Liber Pontificalis,* ed. Ernest Thorin, 2 vols., Paris, 1886–1892.

Fagnanus, Prosper, *Commentaria in Quinque Libros Decretalium,* 4 vols., Venetiis, 1697.

Fanfani, Ludovicus, *De Indulgentiis,* ed. altera, notabiliter aucta, Romae: Marietti, 1926.

————, *De Iure Parochorum,* Taurini-Romae: Marietti, 1924.

Ferraris, Lucius, *Bibliotheca Canonica, Iuridica, Moralis Theologica nec non Ascetica, Polemica, Rubricistica, Historica,* 9 vols., Romae, 1885–1899.

Ferreres, Ioannes, *Institutiones Canonicae,* 2. ed., 2 vols., Barcinone: Eugenius Subirana, 1920.

Gasparri, Petrus, *Tractus Canonicus de Sacra Ordinatione,* 2 vols., Parisiis, 1893–1894.

Godfrey, John, *The Right of Patronage According to the Code of Canon Law,*

The Catholic University of America Canon Law Studies, n. 21, Washington, D.C.: The Catholic University of America, 1924.

Hagedorn, Francis, *General Legislation on Indulgences*, The Catholic University of America Canon Law Studies, n. 22, Washington, D.C.: The Catholic University of America, 1924.

Hervé, J. M., *Manuale Theologiae Dogmaticae*, 4 vols., Parisiis: Berche et Pagis, 1934–1936. Vol. I, 18. ed., 1934; Vol. II, 17. ed., 1934; Vol. III, 17. ed., 1935; Vol. IV, 16. ed., 1936.

Hilling, Nicolaus, *Das Personenrecht des Codex Iuris Canonici*, Paderborn: Schöningh, 1924.

Hinschius, Paul, *Das Kirchenrecht der Katholiken und Protestanten in Deutschland*, 6 vols., Berlin, 1869–1897.—Vols. I–IV, *System des Katholischen Kirchenrechts*, Berlin, 1869–1888.

Hostiensis, Cardinalis (Henricus de Segusio), *In Decretalium Libros Commentaria*, 5 vols. in 3, Venetiis, 1581.

Jaeger, Leo, *The Administration of Vacant and Quasi-vacant Episcopal Sees in the United States*, The Catholic University of America Canon Law Studies, n. 81, Washington, D.C.: The Catholic University of America, 1932.

Jone, Heribert, *Gesetzbuch des kanonischen Rechtes*, 3 vols., Paderborn: Ferdinand Schöningh, 1939–1941. Vol. I, 1939; Vol. II, 1940; Vol. III, 1941.

Keene, Michael, *Religious Ordinaries and Canon 198*, The Catholic University of America Canon Law Studies, n. 135, Washington, D.C.: The Catholic University of America Press, 1942.

Knowles, David, *The Monastic Order in England*, Cambridge: The University Press, 1941.

Köstler, Rudolf, *Wörterbuch zum Codex Iuris Canonici*, München: Verlag Josef Kosel & Friedrich Pustet, 1927–1929.

Lega, Michael–Bartoccetti, Victor, *Commentarius in Iudicia Ecclesiastica*, 3 vols., Romae: Anonima Libraria Cattolica Italiana, 1938–1941.

Lexikon für Theologie und Kirche, 10 vols., Freiburg im B.: Herder & Co., 1930–1938.

Martinucci, Pius, *Manuale Sacrarum Caeremoniarum*, 3. ed., II partes in IV vols., Ratisbonae: Pustet, 1911–1915.

Migne, Jacques, *Patrologiae Cursus Completus, Series Latina*, 221 vols., Parisiis, 1858–1864.

Moeder, John, *The Proper Bishop for Ordination and Dimissorial Letters*, The Catholic University of America Canon Law Studies, n. 95, Washington, D.C.: The Catholic University of America, 1935.

Molitor, Raphael, *Religiosi Iuris Capita Selecta*, Ratisbonae, 1909.

Munerati, Dantes, *Iuris Ecclesiastici Publici et Privati Elementa*, 4. ed., Romae: Ex Schola Typographica Salesiana, 1926.

McBride, James, *Incardination and Excardination of Seculars*, The Catholic University of America Canon Law Studies, n. 145, Washington, D.C.: The Catholic University of America Press, 1941.

McDevitt, Gilbert, *Legitimacy and Legitimation*, The Catholic University of America Canon Law Studies, n. 138, Washington, D.C.: The Catholic University of America Press, 1941.

Oesterle, Gerardus, *Praelectiones Iuris Canonici* (manuscripti instar), Romae: Collegio S. Anselmi, 1931.

Ojetti, Benedictus, *Synopsis Rerum Moralium et Iuris Pontificii*, Romae, 1899.

Ottaviani, Alaphridus, *Institutionis Iuris Publici Ecclesiastici*, 2 vols., Typis Polyglottis Vaticanis, 1935–1936.

Pallottini, Salvator, *Collectio omnium conclusionum et resolutionum quae in causis propositis apud Sacram Congregationem Cardinalium S. Concilii Tridentini Interpretum prodierunt ab eius institutione anno MCLXIV ad annum MDCCCLX, distinctis titulis alphabetico ordine per materias digesta*, 17 vols., Romae, 1868–1893.

Parsons, Anscar, *Canonical Elections*, The Catholic University of America Canon Law Studies, n. 118, Washington, D.C.: The Catholic University of America Press, 1939.

Pejška, Josephus, *Ius Canonicum Religiosorum*, 3. ed., Friburgi Brisgoviae: Herder & Co., 1927.

Petra, Vincentius, *Commentaria ad Constitutiones Apostolicas*, 5 vols. in 2, Venetiis, 1729.

Pistocchi, Marius, *De Re Beneficiali*, Taurini (Italia): Marietti, 1928.

Pontificale Romanum, Mechliniae: Dessain, 1895.

Prümmer, Dominicus, *Manuale Iuris Canonici*, 6. ed., Friburgi Brisgoviae: Herder & Co., 1933.

Reiffenstuel, Anacletus, *Jus Canonicum Universum*, 6 vols. in 5, Romae, 1831–1835.

Roberti, Franciscus, *De Processibus*, Vol. I, 2. ed., Romae: Apud aedes Facultatis Juridicae ad S. Apollinaris, (1941?).

Schmalzgrueber, Franciscus, *Jus Ecclesiasticum Universum*, 5 vols. in 12, Romae, 1843–1845.

Schaefer, Timotheus, *De Religiosis*, 3. ed., Romae: Herder, 1940.

Schroeder, H. J., *Canons and Decrees of the Council of Trent*, St. Louis, Mo.: B. Herder Book Co., 1941.

Tamburini, Ascanius, *De Jure Abbatum et Aliorum Praelatorum tam Regularium, quam Secularium Episcopis Inferiorum*, 3 vols., Coloniae Agrippinae, 1691.

Thomas, Aquinas, St., *Opera Omnia*, studio ac labore Stanislai Eduardi Fretté et Pauli Maré, 34 vols., Parisiis, 1872–1880.

Thomassinus, Ludovicus, *Vetus et Nova Ecclesiae Disciplina*, 10 vols., Magontiaci, 1787.

Toso, Albertus, *Ad Codicem Iuris Canonici Commentaria Minora*, 3 vols. in 1. Vol. I, Tiferni Tiberini: Typogr. Vinciana, 1921; Vol. II, Romae, Ephemeridis *Jus Pontificium* cura et impensis, 1923; Vol. III, pars I, Romae: *Jus Pontificium*, Piazza SS. Apostoli, 1925; Vol. III, pars II, Romae: *Jus Pontificium*, Piazza SS. Apostoli, 1927.

Trombetta, Aloysius, *De Consensu et Consilio Capituli Cathedralis iuxta Codicem Iuris Canonici*, Neapoli: M. D'Auria, 1926.

Vermeersch, Arthurus–Creusen, Iosephus, *Epitome Iuris Canonici*, 3 vols., Mechliniae-Romae: H. Dessain, 1934–1937. Vol. I, 6. ed., 1937; Vol. II, 5. ed., 1934; Vol. III, 5. ed., 1936.

Wernz, Franciscus, *Ius Decretalium*, 2. ed., 6 vols., Romae, 1908–1913.

Wernz, F.–Vidal, P., *Ius Canonicum*, 7 toms. in 8 vols., Romae: Apud Aedes Universitatis Gregorianae, 1923–1938.

Woywod, Stanislaus, *A Practical Commentary on the Code of Canon Law*, 5. ed., 2 vols., New York: Joseph F. Wagner, 1939.

Periodicals

Apollinaris, Romae, 1928–.

Archiv für katholisches Kirchenrecht, Innsbruck, 1875–1861; Mainz, 1862–.

Australasian Catholic Record, The, Manly, 1923–.

Commentarium pro Religiosis, Romae, 1920–1934.

Commentarium pro Religiosis et Missionariis, Romae, 1935.–

Ecclesiastical Review, The (Originally *The American Ecclesiastical Review*), Philadelphia, 1889–.

English Historical Review, The, London, 1886–.

Jurist, The, Washington, D.C., 1941–.

Jus Pontificium, Romae, 1921–.

Periodica de Re Canonica et Morali utili praesertim Religiosis et Missionariis, Brugi, 1905–.

Articles

(Anonymous), "Use of Pontificals by Benedictine Abbots,"—*ER*, CVIII (1943), 454–456.

(Anonymous), "Annotationes,"—*Periodica*, XIV (1925), 178–187.

Cappello, F., "De Consecratione Ecclesiarum,"—*Periodica*, XIX (1930), 133*–142*.

Clarke, "The Minister of the Sacrament of Confirmation,"—*The Australasian Catholic Record,* I (1924), n. 2, p. 17–20.

Connell, F., "The Episcopate,"—*ER,* LXXXII (1925), 335–345.

Egerton Beck, "Two Bulls of Boniface IX for the Abbot of St. Osyth," —*EHR,* XXVI (1911), 124–127.

Goyeneche, S., "Consultationes,"—*CpR,* XVIII (1937), 96.

Hergenröther, "Ueber den kirchenrechtlichen Begriff der Nomination,"—*AKKR,* XXXIX (1878), 193–214.

Larraona, A., "Commentarium Codicis,"—*CpR,* IV (1923), 210–218.

Maroto, P., "De Ecclesiae Consecratione,"—*Apollinaris,* IV (1931), 243–250.

Roelker, E. G., "The Vicar General and the Special Mandate,"—*The Jurist,* II (1942), 346–362.

ABBREVIATIONS

AAS—Acta Apostolicae Sedis.

AKKR—Archiv für katholisches Kirchenrecht.

ASS—Acta Sanctae Sedis.

Bull. Ben. XIV—Bullarium Benedicti XIV.

Bull. Rom. Cont.—Bullarii Romani Continuatio.

Bull. Rom. Taur.—Bullarium Romanum, ed. Taurinensis.

Can.—Canon.

CpR—Commentarium pro Religiosis.

CpRM—Commentarium pro Religiosis et Missionariis.

Decr. Auth. S.R.C.—Decreta Authentica Congregationis Sacrorum Rituum.

ER—The Ecclesiastical Review.

EHR—The English Historical Review.

JE—Jaffé-Ewald, *Regesta Pontificum.*

JK—Jaffé-Kaltenbrunner, *Regesta Pontificum.*

JL—Jaffé-Loewenfeld, *Regesta Pontificum.*

MGH—Monumenta Germaniae Historica.

P.C.I.—Pontificia Commissio ad Codicis Canones authentice interpretandos.

S.C.C.—Sacra Congregatio Concilii.

S.C. Consist.—Sacra Congregatio Consistorialis.

S.R.C.—Sacrorum Rituum Congregatio.

S.R.R.—Sacra Romana Rota.

ALPHABETICAL INDEX

BIOGRAPHICAL NOTE

Matthew Aloysius Benko was born on February 24, 1914, at Banning, Fayette county, Pennsylvania. He received his elementary education in St. Benedict's Parochial School, at Marguerite, Pennsylvania. In 1927 he entered Saint Vincent Preparatory School, Latrobe, Pa., and after two years of college training in the same institution he entered the novitiate of the Order of St. Benedict, at Saint Vincent Archabbey, Latrobe, Pa. Here he made his temporary religious profession, which was followed by his solemn profession in 1937. In the fall of 1934 he entered Saint Vincent Seminary where he received his philosophical and theological training, meriting the Bachelor of Arts Degree in 1936, and the Master of Arts Degree in 1938. He was ordained to the priesthood on June 16, 1940. In the autumn of that year he entered the School of Canon Law at the Catholic University of America, where he received the Degree of the Bacculaureate in Canon Law in June, 1941, and the Degree of the Licentiate in Canon Law in June, 1942.

CANON LAW STUDIES*

1. Freriks, Rev. Celestine A., C.PP.S., J.C.D., Religious Congregations in Their External Relations, 121 pp., 1916.
2. Galliher, Rev. Daniel M., O.P., J.C.D., Canonical Elections, 117 pp., 1917.
3. Borkowski, Rev. Aurelius L., O.F.M., J.C.D., De Confraternitatibus Ecclesiasticis, 136 pp., 1918.
4. Castillo, Rev. Cayo, J.C.D., Disertacion Historico-Canonica sobre la Potestad del Cabildo en Sede Vacante o Impedida del Vicario Capitular, 99 pp., 1919 (1918).
5. Kubelbeck, Rev. William J., S.T.B., J.C.D., The Sacred Penitentiaria and Its Relation to Faculties of Ordinaries and Priests, 129 pp., 1918.
6. Petrovits, Rev. Joseph, J.C., S.T.D., J.C.D., The New Church Law on Matrimony, X-461 pp., 1919.
7. Hickey, Rev. John J., S.T.B., J.C.D., Irregularities and Simple Impediments in the New Code of Canon Law, 100 pp., 1920.
8. Klekotka, Rev. Peter J., S.T.B., J.C.D., Diocesan Consultors, 179 pp., 1920.
9. Wanenmacher, Rev. Francis, J.C.D., The Evidence in Ecclesiastical Procedure Affecting the Marriage Bond, 1920 (Printed 1935).
10. Golden, Rev. Henry Francis, J.C.D., Parochial Benefices in the New Code, IV-119 pp., 1921 (Printed 1925).
11. Koudelka, Rev. Charles J., J.C.D., Pastors, Their Rights and Duties According to the New Code of Canon Law, 211 pp., 1921.
12. Melo, Rev. Antonius, O.F.M., J.C.D., De Exemptione Regularium, X-188 pp., 1921.
13. Schaaf, Rev. Valentine Theodore, O.F.M., S.T.B., J.C.D., The Cloister, X-180 pp., 1921.
14. Burke, Rev. Thomas Joseph, S.T.D., J.C.D., Competence in Ecclesiastical Tribunals, IV-117 pp., 1922.
15. Leech, Rev. George Leo, J.C.D., A Comparative Study of the Constitution "Apostolicae Sedis" and the "Codex Juris Canonici," 179 pp., 1922.
16. Motry, Rev. Hubert Louis, S.T.D., J.C.D., Diocesan Faculties According to the Code of Canon Law, II-167 pp., 1922.
17. Murphy, Rev. George Lawrence, J.C.D., Delinquencies and Penalties in the Administration and the Reception of the Sacraments, IV-121 pp., 1923.
18. O'Reilly, Rev. John Anthony, S.T.B., J.C.D., Ecclesiastical Sepulture in the New Code of Canon Law, II-129 pp., 1923.

* Below n. 100 only the following numbers are still available: Nn. 3, 4, 9, 25, 34, 57 and 75. Beginning with n. 100 only the following are unavailable: Nn. 100, 101, 102, 104, 105, 107, 108, 109, 111 and 113.

19. Michalicka, Rev. Wenceslas Cyrill, O.S.B., J.C.D., Judicial Procedure in Dismissal of Clerical Exempt Religious, 107 pp., 1923.
20. Dargin, Rev. Edward Vincent, S.T.B., J.C.D., Reserved Cases According to the Code of Canon Law, IV-103 pp., 1924.
21. Godfrey, Rev. John A., S.T.B., J.C.D., The Right of Patronage According to the Code of Canon Law, 153 pp., 1924.
22. Hagedorn, Rev. Francis Edward, J.C.D., General Legislation on Indulgences, II-154 pp., 1924.
23. King, Rev. James Ignatius, J.C.D., The Administration of the Sacraments to Dying Non-Catholics, V-141 pp., 1924.
24. Winslow, Rev. Francis Joseph, O.F.M., J.C.D., Vicars and Prefects Apostolic, IV-149 pp., 1924.
25, Correa, Rev. Jose Servelion, S.T.L., J.C.D., La Potestad Legislativa de la Iglesia Catolica, IV-127 pp., 1925.
26. Dugan, Rev. Henry Francis, A.M., J.C.D., The Judiciary Department of the Diocesan Curia, 87 pp., 1925.
27. Keller, Rev. Charles Frederick, S.T.B., J.C.D., Mass Stipends, 167 pp., 1925.
28. Paschang, Rev. John Linus, J.C.D., The Sacramentals According to the Code of Canon Law, 129 pp., 1925.
29. Piontek, Rev. Cyrillus, O.F.M., S.T.B., J.C.D., De Indulto Exclaustrationis necnon Saecularizationis, XIII-289 pp., 1925.
30. Kearney, Rev. Richard Joseph, S.T.B., J.C.D., Sponsors at Baptism According to the Code of Canon Law, IV-127 pp., 1925.
31. Bartlett, Rev. Chester Joseph, A.M., LL.B., J.C.D., The Tenure of Parochial Property in the United States of America, V-108 pp., 1926.
32. Kilker, Rev. Adrian Jerome, J.C.D., Extreme Unction, V-425 pp., 1926.
33. McCormick, Rev. Robert Emmett, J.C.D., Confessors of Religious, VIII-266 pp., 1926.
34. Miller, Rev. Newton Thomas, J.C.D., Founded Masses According to the Code of Canon Law, VII-93 pp., 1926.
35. Roelker, Rev. Edward G., S.T.D., J.C.D., Principles of Privilege According to the Code of Canon Law, XI-166 pp., 1926.
36. Bakalarczyk, Rev. Richardus, M.I.C., J.U.D., De Novitiatu, VIII-208 pp., 1927.
37. Pizzuti, Rev. Lawrence, O.F.M., J.U.L., De Parochis Religiosis, 1927. (Not Printed.)
38. Bliley, Rev. Nicholas Martin, O.S.B., J.C.D., Altars According to the Code of Canon Law, XIX-132 pp., 1927.
39. Brown, Mr. Brendan Francis, A.B., LL.M., J.U.D., The Canonical Juristic Personality with Special Reference to its Status in the United States of America, V-212 pp., 1927.
40. Cavanaugh, Rev. William Thomas, C.P., J.U.D., The Reservation of the Blessed Sacrament, VIII-101 pp., 1927.
41. Doheny, Rev. William J., C.S.C., A.B., J.U.D., Church Property: Modes of Acquisition, X-118 pp., 1927.

42. Feldhaus, Rev. Aloysius H., C.PP.S., J.C.D., Oratories, IX-141 pp., 1927.
43. Kelly, Rev. James Patrick, A.B., J.C.D., The Jurisdiction of the Simple Confessor, X-208 pp., 1927.
44. Neuberger, Rev. Nicholas J., J.C.D., Canon 6 or the Relation of the Codex Juris Canonici to the Preceding Legislation, V-95 pp., 1927.
45. O'Keefe, Rev. Gerald Michael, J.C.D., Matrimonial Dispensations, Powers of Bishops, Priests, and Confessors, VIII-232 pp., 1927.
46. Quigley, Rev. Joseph A. M., A.B., J.C.D., Condemned Societies, 139 pp., 1927.
47. Zaplotnik, Rev. Johannes Leo, J.C.D., De Vicariis Foraneis, X-142 pp., 1927.
48. Duskie, Rev. John Aloysius, A.B., J.C.D., The Canonical Status of the Orientals in the United States, VIII-196 pp., 1928.
49. Hyland, Rev. Francis Edward, J.C.D., Excommunication, Its Nature, Historical Development and Effects, VIII-181 pp., 1928.
50. Reinmann, Rev. Gerald Joseph, O.M.C., J.C.D., The Third Order Secular of Saint Francis, 201 pp., 1928.
51. Schenk, Rev. Francis J., J.C.D., The Matrimonial Impediments of Mixed Religion and Disparity of Cult, XVI-318 pp., 1929.
52. Coady, Rev. John Joseph, S.T.D., J.U.D., A.M., The Appointment of Pastors, VIII-150 pp., 1929.
53. Kay, Rev. Thomas Henry, J.C.D., Competence in Matrimonial Procedure, VIII-164 pp., 1929.
54. Turner, Rev. Sidney Joseph, C.P., J.U.D., The Vow of Poverty, XLIX-217 pp., 1929.
55. Kearney, Rev. Raymond A., A.B., S.T.D., J.C.D., The Principles of Delegation, VII-149 pp., 1929.
56. Conran, Rev. Edward James, A.B., J.C.D., The Interdict, V-163 pp., 1930.
57. O'Neill, Rev. William H., J.C.D., Papal Rescripts of Favor, VII-218 pp., 1930.
58. Bastnagel, Rev. Clement Vincent, J.U.D., The Appointment of Parochial Adjutants and Assistants, XV-257 pp., 1930.
59. Ferry, Rev. William A., A.B., J.C.D., Stole Fees, V-136 pp., 1930.
60. Costello, Rev. John Michael, A.B., J.C.D., Domicile and Quasi-Domicile, VII-201 pp., 1930.
61. Kremer, Rev. Michael Nicholas, A.B., S.T.B., J.C.D., Church Support in the United States, VI-136 pp., 1930.
62. Angulo, Rev. Luis, C.M., J.C.D., Legislation de la Iglesia sobre la intencion en la application de la Santa Misa, VII-104 pp., 1931.
63. Frey, Rev. Wolfgang Norbert, O.S.B., A.B., J.C.D., The Act of Religious Profession, VIII-174 pp., 1931.
64. Roberts, Rev. James Brendan, A.B., J.C.D., The Banns of Marriage, XIV-140 pp., 1931.
65. Ryder, Rev. Raymond Aloysius, A.B., J.C.D., Simony, IX-151 pp., 1931.

66. Campagna, Rev. Angelo, Ph.D., J.U.D., Il Vicario Generale del Vescovo, VII-205 pp., 1931.
67. Cox, Rev. Joseph Godfrey, A.B., J.C.D., The Administration of Seminaries, VI-124 pp., 1931.
68. Gregory, Rev. Donald J., J.U.D., The Pauline Privilege, XV-165 pp., 1931.
69. Donohue, Rev. John F., J.C.D., The Impediment of Crime, VII-110 pp., 1931.
70. Dooley, Rev. Eugene A., O.M.I., J.C.D., Church Law on Sacred Relics, IX-143 pp., 1931.
71. Orth, Rev. Clement Raymond, O.M.C., J.C.D., The Approbation of Religious Institutes, 171 pp., 1931.
72. Pernicone, Rev. Joseph M., A.B., J.C.D., The Ecclesiastical Prohibition of Books, XII-267 pp., 1932.
73. Clinton, Rev. Connell, A.B., J.C.D., The Paschal Precept, IX-108 pp., 1932.
74. Donnelly, Rev. Francis B., A.M., S.T.L., J.C.D., The Diocesan Synod, VIII-125 pp., 1932.
75. Torrente, Rev. Camilo, C.M.F., J.C.D., Las Processiones Sagradas, V-145 pp., 1932.
76. Murphy, Rev. Edwin J., C.PP.S., J.C.D., Suspension Ex Informata Conscientia, XI-122 pp., 1932.
77. MacKenzie, Rev. Eric F., A.M., S.T.L., J.C.D., The Delict of Heresy in its Commission, Penalization, Absolution, VII-124 pp., 1932.
78. Lyons, Rev. Avitus E., S.T.B., J.C.D., The Collegiate Tribunal of First Instance, XI-147 pp., 1932.
79. Connolly, Rev. Thomas A., J.C.D., Appeals, XI-195 pp., 1932.
80. Sangmeister, Rev. Joseph V., A.B., J.C.D., Force and Fear as Precluding Matrimonial Consent, V-211 pp., 1932.
81. Jaeger, Rev. Leo A., A.B., J.C.D., The Administration of Vacant and Quasi-Vacant Episcopal Sees in the United States, IX-229 pp., 1932.
82. Rimlinger, Rev. Herbert T., J.C.D., Error Invalidating Matrimonial Consent, VII-79 pp., 1932.
83. Barrett, Rev. John D. M., S.S., J.D.C., A Comparative Study of the Third Plenary Council of Baltimore and the Code, IX-221 pp., 1932.
84. Carberry, Rev. John J., Ph.D., S.T.D., J.C.D., The Juridical Form of Marriage, X-177 pp., 1934.
85. Dolan, Rev. John L., A.B., J.C.D., The Defensor Vinculi, XII-157 pp., 1934.
86. Hannan, Rev. Jerome D., A.M., S.T.D., LL.B., J.C.D., The Canon Law of Wills, IX-517 pp., 1934.
87. Lemieux, Rev. Delise A., A.M., J.C.D., The Sentence in Ecclesiastical Procedure, IX-133 pp., 1934.
88. O'Rourke, Rev. James J., A.B., J.C.D., Parish Registers, VII-109 pp., 1934.

89. Timlin, Rev. Bartholomew, O.F.M., A.M., J.C.D., Conditional Matrimonial Consent, X-381 pp., 1934.
90. Wahl, Rev. Francis X., A.B., J.C.D., The Matrimonial Impediments of Consanguinity and Affinity, VI-125 pp., 1934.
91. White, Rev. Robert J., A.B., LL.B., S.T.B., J.C.D., Canonical Ante-Nuptial Promises and the Civil Law, VI-152 pp., 1934.
92. Herrera, Rev. Antonio Parra, O.C.D., J.C.D., Legislacion Ecclesiastica sobra el Ayuno y la Abstinencia, XI-191 pp., 1935.
93. Kennedy, Rev. Edwin J., J.C.D., The Special Matrimonial Process in Cases of Evident Nullity, X-165 pp., 1935.
94. Manning, Rev. John J., A.B., J.C.D., Presumption of Law in Matrimonial Procedure, XI-111 pp., 1935.
95. Moeder, Rev. John M., J.C.D., The Proper Bishop for Ordination and Dimissorial Letters, VII-135 pp., 1935.
96. O'Mara, Rev. William A., A.B., J.C.D., Canonical Causes for Matrimonial Dispensations, IX-155 pp., 1935.
97. Reilly, Rev. Peter, J.C.D., Residence of Pastors, IX-81 pp., 1935.
98. Smith, Rev. Mariner T., O.P., S.T.Lr., J.C.D., The Penal Law for Religious, VII-169 pp., 1935.
99. Whalen, Rev. Donald W., A.M., J.C.D., The Value of Testimonial Evidence in Matrimonial Procedure, XIII-297 pp., 1935.
100. Cleary, Rev. Joseph F., J.C.D., Canonical Limitations on the Alienation of Church Property, VIII-141 pp., 1936.
101. Glynn, Rev. John C., J.C.D., The Promoter of Justice, XX-337 pp., 1936.
102. Brennan, Rev. James H., S.S., M.A., S.T.B., J.C.D., The Simple Convalidation of Marriage, VI-135 pp., 1937.
103. Brunini, Rev. Joseph Bernard, J.C.D., The Clerical Obligations of Canons 139 and 142, X-121 pp., 1937.
104. Connor, Rev. Maurice, A.B., J.C.D., The Administrative Removal of Pastors, VIII-159 pp., 1937.
105. Guilfoyle, Rev. Merlin Joseph, J.C.D., Custom, XI-144 pp., 1937.
106. Hughes, Rev. James Austin, A.B., A.M., J.C.D., Witnesses in Criminal Trial of Clerics, IX-140 pp., 1937.
107. Jansen, Rev. Raymond J., A.B., S.T.L., J.C.D., Canonical Provisions for Catechetical Instruction, VII-153 pp., 1937.
108. Kealy, Rev. John James, A.B., J.C.D., The Introductory Libellus in Church Court Procedure, XI-121 pp., 1937.
109. McManus, Rev. James Edward, C.SS.R., J.C.D., The Administration of Temporal Goods in Religious Institutes, XVI-196 pp., 1937.
110. Moriarty, Rev. Eugene James, J.C.D., Oaths in Ecclesiastical Courts, X-115 pp., 1937.
111. Rainer, Rev. Eligius George, C.SS.R., J.C.D., Suspension of Clerics, XVII-249 pp., 1937.
112. Reilly, Rev. Thomas F., C.SS.R., J.C.D., Visitation of Religious, VI-195 pp., 1938.

113. Moriarty, Rev. Francis E., C.SS.R., J.C.D., The Extraordinary Absolution from Censures, XV-334 pp., 1938.
114. Connolly, Rev. Nicholas P., J.C.D., The Canonical Erection of Parishes, X-132 pp., 1938.
115. Donovan, Rev. James Joseph, J.C.D., The Pastor's Obligation in Prenuptial Investigation, XII-322 pp., 1938.
116. Harrigan, Rev. Robert J., M.A., S.T.B., J.C.D., The Radical Sanation of Invalid Marriages, VIII-208 pp., 1938.
117. Boffa, Rev. Conrad Humbert, J.C.D., Canonical Provisions for Catholic Schools, VII-211 pp., 1939.
118. Parsons, Rev. Anscar John, O.M.Cap., J.C.D., Canonical Elections, XII-236 pp., 1939.
119. Reilly, Rev. Edward Michael, A.B., J.C.D., The General Norms of Dispensation, XII-156 pp., 1939.
120. Ryan, Rev. Gerald Aloysius, A.B., J.C.D., Principles of Episcopal Jurisdiction, XII-172 pp., 1939.
121. Burton, Rev. Francis James, C.S.C., A.B., J.C.D., A Commentary on Canon 1125, X-222 pp., 1940.
122. Miaskiewicz, Rev. Francis Sigismund, J.C.D., Supplied Jurisdiction According to Canon 209, XII-340 pp., 1940.
123. Rice, Rev. Patrick William, A.B., J.C.D., Proof of Death in Prenuptial Investigation, VIII-156 pp., 1940.
124. Anglin, Rev. Thomas Francis, M.S., J.C.D., The Eucharistic Fast, VIII-183 pp., 1941.
125. Coleman, Rev. John Jerome, J.C.D., The Minister of Confirmation, VI-153 pp., 1941.
126. Downs, Rev. Joseph Emmanuel, A.B., J.C.D., The Concept of Clerical Immunity, XI-163 pp., 1941.
127. Esswein, Rev. Anthony Albert, J.C.D., Extrajudicial Penal Powers of Ecclesiastical Superiors, X-144 pp., 1941.
128. Farrell, Rev. Benjamin Francis, M.A., S.T.L., J.C.D., The Rights and Duties of the Local Ordinary Regarding Congregations of Women Religious of Pontifical Approval, V-195 pp., 1941.
129. Feeney, Rev. Thomas John, A.B., S.T.L., J.C.D., Restitutio in Integrum, VI-169 pp., 1941.
130. Findlay, Rev. Stephen William, O.S.B., A.B., J.C.D., Canonical Norms Governing the Deposition and Degradation of Clerics, XVII-279 pp., 1941.
131. Goodwine, Rev. John, A.B., S.T.L., J.C.D., The Right of the Church to Acquire Property, VIII-119 pp., 1941.
132. Heston, Rev. Edward Louis, C.S.C., Ph.D., S.T.D., J.C.D., The Alienation of Church Property in the United States, XII-222 pp., 1941.
133. Hogan, Rev. James John, A.B., S.T.L., J.C.D., Judicial Advocates and Procurators, XIII-200 pp., 1941.
134. Kealy, Rev. Thomas M., A.B., Litt.B., J.C.D., Dowry of Women Religious, IX-152 pp., 1941.

135. Keene, Rev. Michael James, O.S.B., J.C.D., Religious Ordinaries and Canon 198, V-164 pp., 1942.
136. Kerin, Rev. Charles A., S.S., M.A., S.T.B., J.C.D., The Privation of Christian Burial, XVI-279 pp., 1941.
137. Louis, Rev. William Francis, M.A., J.C.D., Diocesan Archives, X-101 pp., 1941.
138. McDevitt, Rev. Gilbert Joseph, A.B., J.C.D., Legitimacy and Legitimation, X-247 pp., 1941.
139. McDonough, Rev. Thomas Joseph, A.B., J.C.D., Apostolic Administrators, X-217 pp., 1941.
140. Meier, Rev. Carl Anthony, A.B., J.C.D., Penal Administrative Procedure Against Negligent Pastors, XI-240 pp., 1941.
141. Schmidt, Rev. John Rogg, A.B., J.C.D., The Principles of Authentic Interpretation in Canon 17 of the Code of Canon Law, XII-331pp., 1941.
142. Slafkosky, Rev. Andrew Leonard, A.B., J.C.D., The Canonical Episcopal Visitation of the Diocese, X-197 pp., 1941.
143. Swoboda, Rev. Innocent Robert, O.F.M., J.C.D., Ignorance in Relation to the Imputability of Delicts, IX-271 pp., 1941.
144. Dubé, Rev. Arthur Joseph, A.B., J.C.D., The General Principles for the Reckoning of Time in Canon Law, VIII-299 pp., 1941.
145. McBride, Rev. James T., A.B., J.C.D., Incardination and Excardination of Seculars, XX-585 pp., 1941.
146. Król, Rev. John T., J.C.D., The Defendant in Ecclesiastical Trials, XII-207 pp., 1942.
147. Comyns, Rev. Joseph J., C.SS.R., A.B., J.C.D., Papal and Episcopal Administration of Church Property, XIV-155 pp., 1942.
148. Barry, Rev. Garrett Francis, O.M.I., J.C.L., Violation of the Cloister, XII-260 pp., 1942.
149. Bolduc, Rev. Gatien, C.S.V., A.B., S.T.L., J.C.L., Les Études dans les Religions Cléricales.
150. Boyle, Rev. David John, M.A., J.C.D., The Juridic Effects of Moral Certitude on Pre-Nuptial Guarantees, XII-188 pp., 1942.
151. Canavan, Rev. Walter Joseph, M.A., Litt.D., J.C.D., The Profession of Faith, XII-143 pp., 1942.
152. Desrochers, Rev. Bruno, A.B., Ph.L., S.T.B., J.C.D., Le Premier Concile Plénier de Québec et le Code de Droit Canonique, XIV-186 pp., 1942.
153. Dillon, Rev. Robert Edward, A.B., J.C.D., Common Law Marriage, X-148 pp., 1942.
154. Dodwell, Rev. Edward John, Ph.D., S.T.B., J.C.L., The Time and Place for the Celebration of Marriage.
155. Donnellan, Rev. Thomas Andrew, A.B., J.C.D., The Obligation of the Missa pro Populo, VII-131 pp., 1942.
156. Eltz, Rev. Louis Anthony, A.B., J.C.L., Cooperation in Crime.

157. Gass, Rev. Sylvester Francis, M.A., J.C.D., Ecclesiastical Pensions, XI-206 pp., 1942.
158. Guiniven, Rev. John Joseph, C.SS.R., J.C.D., The Precept of Hearing Mass, XIV-188 pp., 1942.
159. Gulczynski, Rev. John Theophilus, J.C.L., The Desecration and Violation of Churches.
160. Hammill, Rev. John Leo, M.A., J.C.D., The Obligations of the Traveler According to Canon 14, VIII-204 pp., 1942.
161. Haydt, Rev. John Joseph, A.B., J.C.D., Reserved Benefices, XI-148 pp., 1942.
162. Huser, Rev. Roger John, O.F.M., A.B., J.C.L., The Crime of Abortion in Canon Law, XII-187 pp., 1942.
163. Kearney, Rev. Francis Patrick, A.B., S.T.L., J.C.L., The Principles of Canon 1127.
164. Linahen, Rev. Leo James, S.T.L., J.C.D., De Absolutione Complicis In Peccato Turpi, 114 pp., 1942.
165. McCloskey, Rev. Joseph Aloysius, A.B., J.C.D., The Subject of Ecclesiastical Law According to Canon 12, XVII-246 pp., 1942.
166. O'Neill, Rev. Francis Joseph, C.SS.R., J.C.D., The Dismissal of Religious in Temporary Vows, XIII-220 pp., 1942.
167. Prince, Rev. John Edward, A.B., S.T.B., J.C.D., The Diocesan Chancellor, X-136 pp., 1942.
168. Riesner, Rev. Albert Joseph, C.SS.R., J.C.D., Apostates and Fugitives from Religious Institutes, IX-168 pp., 1942.
169. Stenger, Rev. Joseph Bernard, J.C.D., The Mortgaging of Church Property, 186 pp., 1942.
170. Waldron, Rev. Joseph Francis, A.B., J.C.D., The Minister of Baptism, XII-197 pp., 1942.
171. Willett, Rev. Robert Albert, J.C.D., The Probative Value of Documents in Ecclesiastical Trials, X-124 pp., 1942.
172. Woeber, Rev. Edward Martin, M.A., J.C.D., The Interpellations, XII-161 pp., 1942.
173. Benko, Rev. Matthew Aloysius, O.S.B., M.A., J.C.L., The Abbot *Nullius*.
174. Christ, Rev. Joseph James, M.A., S.T.L., J.C.L., Dispensation from Vindicative Penalties.
175. Clancy, Rev. Patrick M. J., O.P., A.B., S.T.Lr., J.C.L., The Local Religious Superior.
176. Clarke, Rev. Thomas James, J.C.L., Parish Societies.
177. Connolly, Rev. John Patrick, S.T.L., J.C.L., Synodal Examiners and Parish Priest Consultors.
178. Drumm, Rev. William Martin, A.B., J.C.L., Hospital Chaplains.
179. Flanagan, Rev. Bernard Joseph, A.B., S.T.L., J.C.L., The Canonical Erection of Religious Houses.
180. Kelleher, Rev. Stephen Joseph, A.B., S.T.B., J.C.L., Discussions with non-Catholics: Canonical Legislation.

181. Lewis, Rev. Gordian, C.P., J.C.L., Chapters in Religious Institutes.
182. Marx, Rev. Adolph, J.C.L., The Declaration of Nullity of Marriages Contracted Outside the Church.
183. Matulenas, Rev. Raymond Anthony, O.S.B., A.B., J.C.L., Communication, A Source of Privileges.
184. O'Leary, Rev. Charles Gerard, C.SS.R., J.C.L., Religious Dismissed After Perpetual Profession.
185. Power, Rev. Cornelius Michael, J.C.L., The Blessing of Cemeteries.
186. Shuhler, Rev. Ralph Vincent, O.S.A., J.C.L., Privileges of Religious to Absolve and Dispense.
187. Ziolkowski, Rev. Thaddeus Stanislaus, A.B., J.C.L., The Consecration and Blessing of Churches.

www.ingramcontent.com/pod-product-compliance
Lightning Source LLC
LaVergne TN
LVHW050222080826
844660LV00012B/454

* 9 7 8 0 8 1 3 2 2 3 6 2 9 *